Albert Venn Dicey

The Privy Council

the Arnold prize essay, 1860

Albert Venn Dicey

The Privy Council
the Arnold prize essay, 1860

ISBN/EAN: 9783337301057

Printed in Europe, USA, Canada, Australia, Japan

Cover: Foto ©Andreas Hilbeck / pixelio.de

More available books at **www.hansebooks.com**

THE PRIVY COUNCIL

The Arnold Prize Essay

1860

BY

ALBERT VENN DICEY, B.C.L.

FELLOW OF ALL SOULS COLLEGE

VINERIAN PROFESSOR OF ENGLISH LAW IN THE UNIVERSITY OF OXFORD

London

MACMILLAN AND CO.

AND NEW YORK

1887

Oxford

PRINTED BY HORACE HART, PRINTER TO THE UNIVERSITY

PREFACE.

This book is merely the Arnold Essay of 1860 republished for the use of students in a new and more convenient form. When I resolved, after some hesitation, to republish an essay which had been long out of print, two courses only were, it was clear, open to me. I might, on the one hand, resume studies which had been laid aside for many years, and re-write my whole account of the Privy Council under the guidance of the new light which during the last quarter of a century has by the labours of Freeman, Stubbs, Gneist, and their followers been thrown on the annals of England. To do this would, however, have involved nothing less than the composition of a new book, and the performance of a task for which more pressing occupations, whilst they leave me the inclination, deny me the time. I might, on the other hand, reprint the essay as what it is—a youthful and immature attempt to sketch out the development of a great institution. This is the course I have actually adopted. The book may, it is hoped, be of some little advantage to students. But the best result which can by possibility flow from its republication is that its very defects may stimulate some person more competent than myself to follow out much farther than I have been able to do, the many interesting enquiries suggested by the history of the Privy Council.

A. V. DICEY.

ALL SOULS COLLEGE, 1887.

SCHEME OF ESSAY.

THE PRIVY COUNCIL.

PART I.

WILLIAM I TO RICHARD II.

THE governments of the middle ages were both more and less despotic than they are painted in the theories of modern writers. Those who conceive the prerogatives of the King to have existed for the sake of the public good, find it impossible to account for the maintenance of many royal rights (such as that of purveyance, or of forcing men to labour in the Crown's service), which tend quite as much to injure as to benefit the people governed. Yet though the advocate of popular liberties finds that his theory will not square with historical facts, the supporter of the Divine right of Kings is no less perplexed by the history of the feudal ages.

The early Plantagenets exercised many powers as beneficial to themselves as they were injurious to their people; but it can scarcely be maintained, that the nobles, who rose again and again in arms against their liege lord, who deposed Richard II, and conspired against the second Edward, knew of any Divine right in

Origin and early idea of the Council.

B

kings, or recognised any duty of passive obedience
in subjects. Those, therefore, who desire to see
the institutions of the middle ages as they existed
in fact, must discard at once the liberal theories
of modern treatises on Constitutional Law, and
the servile loyalty of antiquarian writers living
under James I or Charles II.

Feudal
Monarchs.

The ruler of a feudal Monarchy was the first
of a large body of nobles. In some countries,
such as France or Scotland, his power scarcely
exceeded that of individual barons, while it was
greatly outweighed by the collective might of the
nobility. In England, from the circumstances of
the Norman conquest, the Crown had much higher
authority than in other countries; yet even in
England, the early Norman kings may be considered as the greatest family among the nobility,
rather than as raised high above all their barons.
It was not the weakest of English monarchs who,
on telling a noble that he should 'either go or
hang,' was met by the blunt retort, 'I will
neither go nor hang.' The limits, however, imposed on the royal authority were not, in the
earliest times at least, formed by written laws.
No statutes curbed the prerogative of the Con-

Custom of
taking
advice.

queror, or of William Rufus. Their power was
bounded by customs, but customs supported by
the swords of an aristocracy in arms. Among
these usages was one found in every feudal
Monarchy—that of the interchange of advice

between the King and his nobles. It is, however, of importance not to be misled with regard to this custom, by applying to it the standard of modern notions. A King who is forced to receive advice, means, at the present day, a King who is a King in name alone, who 'reigns but does not govern.' According to the ideas prevailing in the eleventh century, it was rather the King's privilege than his duty to receive counsel from the great men of his kingdom. Their recommendations were not, like the advice of modern Parliaments or Ministers, commands, veiled under a polite name ; they were in the strictest sense counsel. The more powerful the monarch, the more frequent the conventions of his barons. In England these assemblies were constantly held, whilst in France, where the royal power was feeble, they became more and more rare. The reason of this is clear. A feudal monarch had to dread the isolation, not the union, of his liege men. A feudatory who threw off his sovereign's rule, withdrew from his counsels. The Dukes of Burgundy, or Normandy, gradually dropped attendance at the royal court. For once let the barons attend their lord, and his authority was secure, since attendance was an acknowledgement of his sovereign rights, and enabled him to turn against any one too powerful subject, the combined forces of the lesser nobility. Hence it was the right as much as the duty of the King

A right rather than a duty.

to demand counsel; and fully as many precautions
were taken to compel the lieges to give advice
as to force the King to hear it.   Thus the writs
which summon peers to Parliament are demands
made by the King from his lieges, that they will,
on their 'homage and fealty,' or 'homage and
allegiance,' meet him to consult on important
matters ; and attendance was urged on those
summoned, as an imperative duty.   A writ
addressed to the Earl of Arundel, though belong-
ing to a later period of history, well shows both
the claim which the Crown made to counsel, and
the unwillingness of subjects to give it, in times
of danger.   'We have assembled,' runs the summons, 'at this time at our Palace at Westminster,
our Great Council, as ye know well, and wende
for certain ye would be there, afore this, as we
wrote unto you ye should, considering the great
causes for which we called our said council. . . . .
And forasmuch as ye be a great Lord of this our
land, and that your presence is full necessary for
the weal of the said land, we will and charge you
oftimes, right straitly, that in all goodly haste,
after the sight of these our letters ye address you
unto the said council, all excusations set apart
notwithstanding all excusations granted by us
unto you, ... and we will you leave not this,
as you desire to do us singular pleasure, and the
welfare of this our land[1].'

[1] Proceedings of Privy Council, vol. vi. p. 294.

It was only a weak or tyrannical King—a John or a Richard II—who neglected to ask counsel; for the ruler who acted without the advice of his great men distinctly outraged the moral feeling of his day. The various measures taken to insure that the King should affix his great seal through the agency of his Chancellor[1], were originally meant, not to limit the royal power, but to compel that power [2] to be exercised after the King had been advised by his highest legal officer. And one of the complaints against Richard II was the omission to take the advice of the peers. *Neglected only by weak kings.*

The importance attached in the middle ages to communication between a King and his nobles, as between a baron and his vassals, bears directly on the history of the Council. That the King might have advisers, he at times convened as many of his great men—'Magnates,' or 'Notables'—as could attend ; and at all times kept about his person a body of officials, themselves nobles, such as his Marshal, his Justiciary, and his Chancellor. He in fact held at his palace, on a large scale, just such a court as each baron kept up, within smaller limits, in his castle. The nobles, assembled on special occasions by special writs, formed, in combination with the officers of the Court, the 'Great Council,' or 'Common Council' of the realm. The chief advisers of the *Council formed of nobles and officials.* *Great Council and Permanent Council.*

[1] Vide infra.
[2] Conf. 28 Ed. I, 2 Rich. II, Ps. C., Rich. vol. i. p. 87.

Crown, who were permanently about the King, constituted the 'Permanent' or 'Continual' Council, whence, in later times, rose the Privy Council. The difference of names is important, since it shows that in the earliest period of its history the smaller Council was generally contrasted with the greater Councils, not as being private while they were public, but as being permanent or continual[1], whereas they were of their nature temporary. At first, indeed, there was little difference of character between the two Councils. Leading nobles were members of the continual Council, and at the meetings of the great Council the officers of the court occupied a prominent place[2]. The three centuries intervening between the Norman Conquest and the reign of Richard II (1066–1376), are the period during which English institutions assumed a form from which they have never essentially varied. At the end of this period, there is found in existence a Parliament of two Houses, distinct Law Courts, and a Council, with peculiar powers, and distinguishable both from the Law Courts and from the Parliament. With the Council alone the present Essay is directly concerned; but the early history of the Council is nothing else than the account of the gradual process, by which judicial and executive legislative and

[1] Proceedings of P. C. Pref. vol. i. Rot. Parl. vol. i. p. 73.
[2] Proceedings of Privy Council, vol. i. p. 4.

political functions were separated from each other, and assigned to different bodies.

The permanent Council under the early Norman Kings consisted of the great officers of state,— the Chancellor, the great Justiciary, the Lord Treasurer, the Lord Steward, the Chamberlain, the Earl Marshal, the Constable [1], and any other persons whom the King chose to appoint; and of the two Archbishops, who claimed a right to form a part of every Council, public or private. Besides these were present, at times, the Comptroller of the Household, the Chancellor of the Exchequer, the Judges, the King's Serjeant, &c. This body was the 'Aula Regia,' or 'Curia Regis,' a Court which has been described in various and at first sight contradictory terms. Thus it has been called the highest Law Court, the Ministry of the King, a Legislative Assembly, &c. The apparent inconsistency of these descriptions vanishes on closer inspection, and throws great light on mediæval history. For the 'Curia Regis' possessed every attribute which has been ascribed to it. It was the executive. It was also a Law Court. It certainly took part in acts of legislation. Still, at the time of its existence it was no anomaly, since to the men of the eleventh century, not the combination but the severance of judicial and executive powers would have appeared anomalous. The 'Aula Regia' was in

Curia Regia

or Aula Regia.

---

[1] Proceedings of Privy Council, i. Pref.

fact neither more nor less than the Court of
the King ; and he who was at once the ruler and
judge of the whole nation, exercised the powers
which he possessed, either directly (and this he
did to a greater extent than modern students
are apt to suppose), or indirectly, through the
instrumentality of his great officers. Hence the
authority of the 'Curia Regis' was as immense
and as undefined as that of the Monarch.

No distinction originally between Continual Council and Great Council.

If this view be appreciated, many difficulties at
once disappear. For example, distinctions have
been drawn between the powers of the Council
when acting alone, and its powers when combined
with the 'Common Council,' or 'Great Council ;'
between the Council as a legislative body, and
the Council as a Law Court. It can now be
perceived that such nice distinctions are valuable
for purposes of analysis, and have a real signifi-
cation when, as in the latter part of Edward III's
reign, or even earlier, the institutions of the
country assume a settled form: but that when
applied to earlier periods of history they lead to
nothing but confusion, since the interest of the
Council's history consists in the light which is
thrown by it on the growth of distinctions now
familiar to all men ; and the whole worth of this
history is lost if these distinctions, whose formation ought to be pointed out, are assumed always
to have been in existence. One instance suffices
to show the perplexities introduced into this

subject, through describing in modern terms a state of things to which they do not apply. It has been a point vehemently discussed, whether the King's Council (and confusion is frequently much increased by the use of the comparatively modern expression 'Privy Council'), was, or was not, during the reigns of the early Norman Kings, the supreme judicial and legislative body of the realm ; whether, that is to say, the King with his special officers of the 'Curia Regis,' or the King and the body of the nobles, constituted the celebrated 'Courts de More,' held yearly at the three great festivals of the church.

Constitu-
tion of
Curia
Regis.

These assemblies are described in various passages of ancient Chronicles, in the following and similar language. 'Thrice a year,' says one annalist, 'did the King wear his crown, when he was in England: at Christmas and Easter he wore it at Winchester, in Whitsuntide at Westminster, and there were with him all the great men all over England— Archbishops and Bishops, Abbots and Earls, Thanes and Knights[1].'

Court
de More.

'Omnes,' says another chronicler, speaking of the same assemblies, 'cujuscunque professionis Magnates regium edictum arcessebat, ut exterarum gentium legati speciem multitudinis apparatumque deliciarum mirarentur[2].' Or, again, to

---

[1] Chron. Sax. i. p. 190.
[2] Wm. of Malmesbury's Chron.

quote from a third writer, 'Cum gratia Dominicæ Nativitatis omnes regni primores ad Curiam Regis pro more venissent [1].'

Not clearly distinct from it.

These, and other descriptions of the 'Courts de More,' bear out but badly the precise and technical terms in which modern writers speak of these conventions. But they show some important facts. First, that the expression 'Curia Regis' was used vaguely, and might mean either simply the 'King's Court,' or an assembly of nobles, or a meeting of the chief officers of state. Secondly, that the difference between assemblies attended chiefly by the great officers of state, and conventions of the nobility, was not clearly marked. Whence it may be inferred, that while at the 'Courts de More' a large number of nobles were usually convened, yet the royal officials took a leading part in their deliberations, and at other times decided judicial cases without calling in any of the nobility.

Various powers combined in it.

The character of the 'Aula Regia' gradually changed. It is often said to have 'broken up' into three or four other bodies. A more appropriate expression would be, that it developed into other institutions. For the alterations it underwent arose from the influence, not of any external power, but of certain internal forces, which made it divide into different parts. From

[1] Edinburgh Review, xxxv. Lord's Report on Dignity of a Peer.

tho earliest times, particular officers of the 'Aula Regia' had their special duties to perform. Indeed the Constable, the Marshal, &c., did not derive their offices from the 'Aula Regia,' but their seat in the 'Aula Regia' from the fact of possessing certain offices. Thus, tho Marshal or tho Constable, assisted, it may bo supposed, by other members of the Court, attended to military matters; tho Chamberlain to financial concerns; the Chancellor to all questions affecting the royal grants. All business brought before the whole Court would, it might naturally bo expected, be referred by the King to that official under whose department it most fittingly came. This anticipation is confirmed by facts. At an early date, questions of finance were referred to a particular branch of the Court, or, to speak more accurately, to the Court convened at a particular place, and for a special purpose. Hence arose tho court 'ad scaccarium' or the 'Exchequer.' This commission or committee of the whole 'Aula Regia' first dealt with affairs of finance; next, as an immediate consequence of its position, decided suits having reference to the Revenue; and lastly, at a later period, dealt with Civil Suits. By these steps, from the 'Curia Regis' sprang a Law Court, in the modern sense of tho term,—that is, a body which administered justice, according to fixed rules and precedents. The separation of the

[sidenote: Rise from Curia Regis of separate bodies.]

Exchequer from the 'Curia Regis' took place about the same time as the formation of the 'Court of King's Bench' and the 'Court of Common Pleas.' The date at which each of these bodies separated off from the 'Aula Regia' cannot be fixed with precision. The separation was in all probability accomplished not later than 1164–1174, and it may be safely assumed that from the reign of John, these Courts were distinct from each other, as also from the Council.

The rise of the Courts of Law made more definite the position of the Council, but the province of its authority was not marked out in the manner which would seem the most natural to a modern reader. It appears indeed at first sight a reasonable supposition, that the powers given to the Law Courts were taken away from the Council; that, in other words, the Council (which is nothing more than the 'Curia Regis' when separated from the judicial tribunals,) and the Law Courts, occupied distinct provinces. Such an assumption is, nevertheless, confuted by facts. Long after the erection of the Law Courts the Council exercised considerable, though peculiar, judicial authority. This anomaly is easy to explain. The exercise of judicial power is a Royal prerogative. In every law court the King is supposed present. Originally he doubtless really presided, and administered justice,

1. The Law Courts.

surrounded by his court (curia.) The pressure
of business soon made it impossible for him to
perform all his duties in his own person, and he
gradually delegated his authority to the regular
judges. This delegation, however, did not strip
the Crown of its prerogative. Though the King
ordinarily exercised his judicial powers through
judges, who acted according to set laws and
precedents, it was still his right to try suits,
either on his own authority or through the
great men of his Council. It could, indeed,
scarcely be supposed that when the King's
Bench exercised its jurisdiction, as being the
'Curia Regis coram ipso rege,' the King could
not decide causes in that assembly, which was
emphatically the 'Curia Regis.'

This more direct exertion of the King's power 2. The
was naturally and of necessity called into action, Council.
when for any reason the Law Courts were
unable to give justice. They might fail to grant
redress, either because, to use the expressive
words of various ordinances, 'there was too
great might on the one side, and too great
unmight on the other,' or because the grievance
referred to them was one which the technical
rules of law did not meet. In each case the
person aggrieved would naturally apply for aid
to the King and his Council. In both instances
the King would, among other counsellors, specially consult the Chancellor, his great legal

officer. Hence the close connection between the Chancellor and the Council—a connection which, from the effects it produced, requires particular notice. At a period when the 'Aula Regia' still constituted one undivided body, one officer, the Chancellor, had, as his peculiar duty, to affix the great seal[1] to writs, grants, &c. Hence, when the division of powers took place, he became the head of a Court, before which were brought all questions affecting the royal grants. As president of this Court, he may be considered to have exercised a jurisdiction as independent of the King's Council as did the Barons of the Exchequer, or the Justices of the King's Bench. Yet even in his capacity of Common Law Judge, the Chancellor was connected somewhat more closely with the Council than were the other judges, both because the passing of grants was a prerogative kept strictly in the Crown's own hands, on the exercise of which the advice of the whole Council was frequently taken, and because, when the Council caused writs to be issued, it was forced to act through the Chancellor. He, however, occupied another position besides that of Judge in a particular Court. As the greatest legal officer of the realm, after the office of Grand Justiciary was abolished; as an Ecclesiastic consulted by the King on all questions of conscience; as, from his possession of

Connection of Chancery with the Council.

---

[1] Vide infra ii.

the great seal, having knowledge of every grant made by the Crown, he was the Council's most influential Law Officer.

Thus, before he began to exercise an equitable jurisdiction of his own, he must, as may be certainly assumed, have been consulted about every legal matter debated in Council. All therefore who needed redress, which the Law Courts could not afford, brought their complaints, either before the Council, or before the Chancellor, as the Council's highest official. Hence the union between the Chancellor's and the Council's jurisdiction, of which examples are to be found in the following petitions, and others of like character.

6 *Ed. I.* The Abbott and Convent of Bradney pray the King for letters of protection.

Resp. Veniat ad Cancellarium et fiat ei quod graciose fieri potest.

'The Convents of London petition the King to appoint a skilful custos over them.'

Resp. 'Præceptum est Cancellario, quod provideat de idoneo custode.'

8 *Ed. II.* The heirs of Redham petition, &c. Responsum est *per Consilium.* Veniant querentes in Cancellario et habeant breve ibidem executoribus Regine, et mittatur petitio in brevi et mandetur eisdem executoribus, quod ipsis informatis, super contentis in petitione, veniant in Cancel-

lario et ibidem examinetur negotium, et si
inveniatur quod Regina tenetur in arreragiis
contentis, referatur Regi, et Rex faciat jus-
titiam[1].

The last answer quoted has peculiar value.
It exhibits the action of the Council as the
King's advisers, the reference of cases to the
Chancery, and their ultimate decision, at times,
by the King in person: but the clearest view
of the Council's relation to the Chancellor is
given by the ordinance 8 Ed. I. Its main object is 'that no petitions may come before the
King and his Council, but by the hands of his
said Chancellor and other chief Ministers. So
that the King and his Council may, without the
load of other business, attend to the Great business of his realm, and of other foreign Countries.'

Here again the Chancellor is seen acting as a
member of the Council; and the language of the
Proclamation suggests the reason of the change,
which, before the reign of Richard II, had taken
place in the relative positions of the great law
officer, and the deliberative body to which it
belonged. As the Law Courts had branched off
from the 'Curia Regis,' so the Chancery began
Gradual   to separate from the Council. The exact steps,
separation. by which the process of separation was carried
out, cannot be known. But it may readily be
supposed that the pressure of other business, and

[1] Campbell's Lives of the Chancellors, vol. i. 187, 206.

a distaste to the niceties of legal discussion,
made the Council glad to first refer matters
of law to the Chancellor, and next to leave them
entirely to his decision. Whatever the steps of
the change, a great alteration took place, and
before the death of Edward III, the Chancellor
decided matters of equity on his own authority,
and gave assistance to those hindered by
violence from obtaining aid through the regular
course of law. The date of his establishment as
a Judge of Equity is approximately marked by
a proclamation of Edward III[1], which referred
matters of grace to the Chancellor's decision.
Though, from about this date, the Chancellor exercised an independent jurisdiction, the Council's
power suffered no diminution. Both the Council and the Chancellor aided those whom
Common Law was unable to protect. Both the
Chancellor and the Council enforced obligations
binding in conscience though not in law.
Attacks made on the power of the Chancellor are
attacks on the authority of the Council,—and
the Council in Chancery can hardly be distinguished from the Chancellor's own Court[2].

Doubts, it is true, have been raised as to how
far the Council possessed originally any extraordinary jurisdiction. The ground on which
they chiefly rest is, that no proof can be found

---

[1] Story's Equity Jurisprudence, s. 44, and notes.
[2] Hallam's Mid. Ages, iii. (12th ed.) pp. 242-261.

that such a jurisdiction was ever exercised
earlier than the reign of Henry III. It is,
however, hard to believe that the Council's
powers were less extensive in an age when the
Crown's prerogative was unrestrained, than at
a time when the regal authority had sensibly
declined; that the counsellors of the third Henry
attempted to exert powers unknown to the
advisers of William I. If the view taken in the
present Essay of the Council's history be correct,
it sufficiently explains the apparent anomaly, of
the Council's authority appearing to increase, at
the very period when it might have been expected to have decreased.

Effected before reign of Henry III. The establishment of the Law Courts, which
had been effected before the time of Henry III,
marked off the Council as a separate body.
Hence powers unnoticed when exercised by the
King himself in the 'Curia Regis,' attract
attention when put forth in acts of the Council.

It was not, however, the exertion of judicial
authority by the King's ministers which was
the novelty. What change there was, consisted
in the rise of the Law Courts. It is, indeed,
admitted that no complaints are heard of the
Council's power till 1331 (5 Ed. III, Cap. 9);
and did the complaints arise earlier, they would
not prove the Council's authority to have been
increased; for an ancient institution is more
generally assailed because men's feelings have

undergone a change, than because of any alteration in its own character. A change of public
sentiment caused the attack on the Council.
The contemporaries of the Conqueror saw
nothing irregular in the exercise of an arbitrary
justice by the King and his courtiers. The
subjects of Edward III, accustomed as they were
to the regular administration of law, beheld in
the Council and the Law Courts the contrast
between irresponsible power and legal authority.
In attacking the former, they dreamed that they
were asserting old privileges, whilst they were
in reality struggling for new rights.

The alteration in men's feelings was closely The
connected with the growth of Parliamentary Council
and the
power. The 'Continual Council' did not Parliament.
originally (as has been mentioned) differ essentially in character from the Great Council.
The King could do nearly every act in his
permanent Council of great men, which he
could perform when surrounded by a larger
number of his nobles; except impose taxes on
these nobles themselves. But to the immediate
successors of the Conqueror, this exception was
of small consequence; since the domain lands,
the regular reliefs, the tallages from the Crown's
tenants, and unlimited exactions from the
Boroughs, afforded a sufficient revenue. In the
course of years the nature both of the 'Common
Councils' of the realm, and of the 'Continual

Council,' altered. The 'Great Council' became, when combined with the Commons, a national convention, in no sense coinciding with the

Changed position of Council and Parliament.
Council; whilst the latter body ceased to be the King's Court, which included within itself nearly all the men of importance who surrounded the King; and tended more and more to become a separate assembly of officials, bound by a particular oath, paid a regular salary, and meeting under precise rules. The steps by which these changes were brought about cannot be separately marked; but, whilst the rise of the House of Commons marks the transition of the 'Common Council' into a Parliament, smaller but as certain signs indicate the Council's altered position. Thus in Edward II's reign appears a Clerk of the Council; in the Statute 29 Ed. I, the names of the King's Principal Counsellors are mentioned, whilst, in various acts, the Council is referred to, almost as a separate Estate of the realm[1].

For example, the Statute 3 Ed. I, 1275, is said to be, 'by his Council,' and by the assent of the Archbishops, Bishops, Nobles, Peers, Lords, Barons, and all the commonalty of the realm. The statute 4 Ed. I is enacted in the 'presence of certain Reverend Fathers, Bishops of England, and others of the King's Council.' In the eighth year of Edward II, appear four

[1] Conf. Hallam's Middle Ages, iii. (12th ed.) p. 143.

petitions to the King and his Council, of which one proceeds from the Lords alone, another from the Commons, and two from the Lords and Commons conjointly. The fact that the Council was assuming the nature of a distinct body is further proved by the appointment early in the reign of Edward III of receivers of petitions for the Council.

Under these circumstances, Parliament natu-rally desired to control the powers of the Council. The wish, natural in itself, was greatly stimu-lated by the influence of the Common Law lawyers, a class of men whose influence was great in Parliament, and who looked with ever increasing jealousy on the 'Doctors of Civil Law,' whose stronghold was the Chancery and the Council. The Council's authority might be depressed by two different ways of proceeding. The appointment of its members might be taken out of the hands of the Crown. If this were done, the powers of the Council might be left unimpaired, or even be increased; since they would be curbed by the assembly who appointed the Councillors. It was possible also to leave the appointment of advisers to the King, but to curtail the authority of the Council. Both courses were tried. The irregular nomination of the Council of Twenty-four Barons, under Henry III, and of the 'Lords Ordainers' under Edward II, are attempts on the part of the

Causes of the contest between them.

'Great Council' to appropriate to itself the right of appointing the 'Permanent Council'; whilst the Acts 5 Ed. III, 25 Ed. III, 28 Ed. III, 42 Ed. III, mark the more moderate endeavours of Parliament to control a body in whose appointment they claimed no share. These bear witness to the influence of Common Law lawyers; since they are manifestly intended to do away with all legal proceedings except those in the Common Law Courts; and first at this period the two influences of 'the Courts' and 'the Parliament,' which have between them ruled the whole history of the Council, unite in the attempt to curb its authority, and, in so doing, to restrain the prerogative of the Crown.

Measures of Parliament.

That the members of the 'Curia Regis' made part of the 'Great Council' is implied in the character of that assembly. But the relations subsisting between the Council and the House of Lords, is not easy to discover. The manner in which the Council's assent to statutes is mentioned suggests that, during the reigns of the two first Edwards, it voted as a separate body. It is certain, however, that under Edward III, whenever the Peers were assembled, the King's Officers sat with them; at first, perhaps, with the right of voting, but later as mere advisers.

Council and House of Lords.

In any sketch of the Council's rise, it is

impossible not to dwell almost exclusively on those circumstances which limited its power; for these limitations are what mark it off as a separate institution. Yet no conception of the Council is more false than that which paints it as a body perpetually encroaching on the rights of the Parliament, or of the Law Courts; and perpetually checked in its encroachments. Altera- Daily tions in the sphere of the Council's authority influence of Council. took place; but their source will be found not in the Council's encroachments, but in the rise of new ideas, such as the conception of fixed laws; or in the growth of new institutions, such as the Parliament or the Law Courts. In looking at the extraordinary exertions of authority, which alone were disputed, the historian ought not to forget the daily exercise of its authority, which, because it was usual, was therefore unnoticed. This error is the more likely to be committed, as no records of the Council's proceedings exist of an earlier date than 1386. It may, indeed, be confidently pronounced, that, before this period, the Council exerted a great influence over all the affairs of State; but the exact nature of this influence, and the manner in which it was employed, must remain a matter of conjecture.

With the reign of Richard II the Council's period of growth closes. Before he reached the throne, the character of English institutions had

become permanently fixed. The vagueness
which marked the constitution of the 'Curia
Regis' had passed away. The Law Courts had
become distinct bodies. The Court of Chancery,
though till a later period closely connected with
the Council, was tending rapidly to become a
separate Court of Equity. The 'Great Councils'
(though still frequently convoked) had surren-
dered their most important functions to Parliament, and the Council itself had become the
same body which, in constitution and powers, it
remained for at least a century.

PART II.

RICHARD II TO HENRY VI.

IT seems to be the result of more than of mere Council's acts first recorded from same date. chance, that the earliest existing records of the Council's proceedings date from the reign of Richard II. It has been shown that as early as the latter years of Edward III the Council had begun to occupy a clearly marked position, distinct at once from that of the Law Courts and from that of the Parliament. The conjecture is therefore natural, that the Council's acts were first accurately recorded when its existence as a separate institution was for the first time distinctly recognized.

Whether this supposition be well founded or not, it is certain that it is not till the reign of Richard II that materials are found through which the enquirer can gain a clear conception of the Council's actual constitution, of the grounds of its influence, and of the manner in which its authority was exercised.

From 1386, for a period of about seventy years, it is possible, owing to the existence of published documents, to gain precise information on these and similar points. Printed records make it apparent that what the Council was under Richard II, such it was, in all essential respects, under Henry VI, and, as may be with confidence asserted (though after 1452 the minutes fall short), such it remained till the accession of Henry VII in 1485. Its influence, indeed, greatly varied during the period covered by the printed records, but not its character; and these minutes possess a peculiar value, from the fact that they exhibit the same institution under most diverse circumstances. The Council is seen in action during the reign of four Monarchs, differing not less in power than in disposition. It is seen as influenced by the tyranny and caprice of Richard,—by the crafty astuteness of Bolingbroke,—by the vigour and success of the victor of Agincourt,—by the piety and imbecility of his son.

Constitution of the Council.

A list[1] of Henry IV's Councillors in 1404, shows them to have formed at that date an assembly of nineteen persons, of whom three are Bishops, nine are Peers, six Knights (mostly persons like Sir T. Espingham, of considerable reputation), and one, a certain John Norbury, whose rank is not marked. This list presents a fair specimen of the class of persons who in general composed the Council. If it is in any way peculiar, it is so by the larger number of

[1] Proceedings of Privy Council, i. 237.

commoners which it contains. The proportion in which different ranks of the community were called upon to specially advise the Crown, constantly varies, and affords a criterion by which to estimate the power of the King and of the feudal aristocracy, respectively. Thus, while under the vigorous administration of Henry IV, many commoners are called to the Council-board; under the feeble rule of his grandson, when factions of the nobility had usurped nearly the whole government, the constantly recurring lists of Councillors contain few untitled names. Under Richard II [1] members of the Council were once at least appointed for a year only; later— and in this change is seen at once a sign and a cause of their increasing influence—their tenure of office (though terminable at the King's pleasure, and at their individual wish[2]), was for the King's life[3]. They were bound by a special oath[4], binding them to ' advise the King according to the best of their cunning and discretion,' to keep the King's counsel secret, and to help in the execution of what should be resolved; and received salaries[5] of large amounts, if the value

Councillors begin to be appointed for life.

[1] Compare 3 Rot. Parl. p. 6.
[2] Compare Regulations of 8 Henry IV. 3 Rot. Parl. p. 572.
[3] See p. 29, *post.*
[4] Steph. Comm. vol. ii. (8th ed.) p. 460.
[5] Proceedings of Privy Council, iii. Preface xix. and p. 154, date 1424. Bishop of Winchester received £200 ; Bishops, Earls, and Treasurer, £132 6s. 4d. ; Barons and Bannerets, £100 ; Squires, £40.

of money in the fifteenth century be taken into account. Their mode of transacting business may be gathered from various ordinances, of which one bearing date 1389 is a sufficient example:—

Mode of transacting business.   'The Council is to meet between eight and nine o'clock. Business of the King's, and of the realm's, is to have precedence over all other matters. Matters relating to the Common Law are to be determined before the Justices. What relates to the office of the Chancellor is to be decided before him. What to the office of the Treasurer, before him in the Exchequer. The King's pleasure is to be ascertained on all matters, which cannot be decided without his special grace. No grants to the detriment of the revenue are to pass without the advice of Council[1].'

King not always present.   These regulations prove that the King was not usually present at the Council's deliberations. His absence is a matter of consequence, since it increased the power of his advisers, and secured their freedom of speech. It is also worth notice that, as is manifested by other ordinances, the Council considered itself so entirely a Law Court as to ordain, that 'out of term-time nothing be sped in the Council, but such thing as for the good of the King and of his land asketh necessary and hasty speed, and may not goodly be abiden into the term-time[2].'

[1] Proceedings of Privy Council, vol. i. p. 18.
[2] Ibid. vol. iii. p. 216.

As regards authority, the Council occupied a Position of position which appears at first sight paradoxical. Council. The same body was at once the controller and the servant of the Crown; the channel through which the royal mandates passed, the instrument of the prerogative; and at the same time the check on the King's power, the curb placed by the aristocracy on the arbitrary exercise of his will. Hence increase in the Council's influence means, at one period of history, a limitation of the prerogative; at another, as for instance in the 16th century, an addition to the royal authority. These seeming inconsistencies are easily reconciled by a consideration of the Council's nature. The Council was nothing more than an assembly of royal officials. It made no claim to independent authority. Its very existence was derived from the King's pleasure, and hence it was dissolved[1], ipso facto by his demise. The Theoretical dependence Council at all times acted in the King's name, on the with a scrupulosity which reaches the height of King. pedantic absurdity, when Henry VI (at the age of five years) is made to assure the Chancellor, that 'if we are negligent in learning[1], or commit any fault, we give our cousin (Earl of Warwick) full power, authority, license, and direction to chastise us, from time to time, according to his discretion, without being impeded or molested by us or any other person, in future, for so doing.'

[1] Steph. Comm. ii. (8th ed.) p. 464.

They treated the King at all times [1] with a cere-
monious etiquette, which sounds servile to
modern ears. The language employed in letters
to Richard II is almost adulatory, and courtesy
is carried to an extreme length, when bound to
inform Henry VI, that a boy of thirteen ought
not to intermeddle in affairs of State [2], aged
ministers begin their lecture with a protest, ' that
it is far from their intention to advise any thing
prejudicial to the King's prerogative, or which
might be a restraint on his liberty or power; and
temper their reproof with the flattering assurance
(of which the latter half was entirely false), that
while knowledge and experience are needed for
affairs of State, ' to this knowledge and feeling,
the King is like, by God's grace, to reach, as soon
as possible by nature, and as has been seen in
any person before his time.'

Under the rule of a vigorous prince, language
of this description was no unmeaning form. It
suited the Council's position. Its members
were powerful administrators, but yet mere
servants of the King's will. Their manner of
transacting business is most curious, and will
require further investigation. Yet looked at as
a mere administrative body, they did not control
the King. Nevertheless they did virtually, in the
ages under consideration, check the royal action,

Practical inde-
pendence
of the
King.

[1] Proceedings of Privy Council, iii. pp. 296–300.
[2] Ibid. iv. p. 287.

so that they became at times not the servants but the 'Ministers,' or even the opponents of their sovereign lord. The circumstances which enabled the Councillors to do this, and the means through which they brought their influence to bear on the Crown, not only directly tell on the Council's history, but are also curious, from their connection with maxims—as for example, that of the 'responsibility of Ministers'—which affect the politics of the present day.

The circumstance which made it possible for the royal advisers to stand in any degree in opposition to the Crown, is that they occupied a position which in fact, though not in theory, made them more than half independent of the Monarch, as regarded their official station. The King could, it is true, appoint or dismiss his advisers, according to his own will. But in the first place, a Council of some kind was a necessity; and secondly, his freedom of choice, though theoretically unfettered, was in practice subject to considerable limitations. Certain officials, as the Marshal, the Chamberlain, necessarily formed part of every Council. Their offices were moreover, in many cases, not in the gift of the Crown, but hereditary in certain families. Further, the presence of a large number of Bishops at the Council-board was unavoidable. For (not to speak of the two Archbishops, who claimed a prescriptive right to be present at all Councils,)

Office of Councillor sometimes hereditary.

Presence of Bishops.

many offices, the chief of which was the Chan-
cellorship, could be filled by none but ecclesiastics.
Which Bishops should be summoned was, it is
true, dependent on the King's choice. But the
presence of men whose main claim to respect the
Crown could not touch, who stood as represen-
tatives of the greatest corporation of the day,
imparted to the Council a dignity and independence which raised it far above a collection of
paid officials.   Further, although the King's
right of appointing Councillors at his pleasure
was unquestioned, it was a prerogative not
unfrequently trenched upon by Parliament. The
deeds of the Lords Appellants under Richard II
may possibly be considered as too revolutionary
a proceeding to give any means of inferring what
could be done legally in ordinary times ; but the
Parliamentary regulations of 1406 [1] show that a
sagacious ruler, such as Henry IV, would at
times suffer the appointment of his advisers to
be wrested out of his hand ; whilst a document
of uncertain date, found amongst the minutes of
his predecessor's reign, exhibits the degree of
independence to which, if the Council never
attained, it at least occasionally aspired. This
' advice of the Lords about the good governance
of the realm ' ordains, amongst other regulations,
' that the King is to allow the Council to exercise

---

[1] Proceedings of Privy Council, i. 295–298, and Rot. Parl. vol.
iii. 585–589. Compare Stubbs, Constitutional Hist. iii. p. 266
(Library Ed.).

their discretion in the government of the kingdom; is to give them audience whenever they wish to communicate with him; is to suffer no one to be reporters between him and the Council, except the Chamberlain, the Steward, or the Keeper of the Privy Seals; is to appoint no Sheriffs or Justices without the advice of the Council[1].'

Whilst the source of the Council's influence over the King is found to be in the independent position of its members, it remains a curious enquiry, What were the means through which this influence made itself felt? The first and most effectual instrument for achieving this object (that indeed into which all subordinate means may be resolved), was the delivery of admonitions and recommendations. The rebukes might be spurned, and the advice neglected; but still the effect produced by counsel, even when unbacked by power, is greater than some modern modes of thought seem to imply. At any rate, the eagerness with which Richard II avoided interviews with his advisers, proves that a tyrannical prince felt their remonstrances a restraint. On this point there is no need for vague conjecture; since an account of a discussion between Richard[2] and his Council gives a picture of the way in which a Monarch's will

Means by which Council influenced King.

Presentation of advice.

---

[1] Proceedings of Privy Council, i. 84.
[2] Ibid. i. 12 b.

might be checked, if not thwarted, by the opposition of his Ministers. The King was anxious to conclude a bargain with the Earl Marshal, for the defence of Berwick. The Council thought the Earl's demands too large, and refused their assent to the agreement. They held at least two conferences with their master, and put forward formally the reasons of their dissent; the most remarkable of which is their fear of being charged in Parliament with having wantonly burdened the revenue. The debate was stormy. The King broke up the first conference ' with a countenance of anger,' and as he withdrew to Kennington, exclaimed, 'Be it at your peril, if any evil come of the delay!' At the second colloquy, a compromise was effected, and the Earl's indentures were signed.

Refusal
to affix
'seals.'

In this dispute the Council apparently refused to affix the 'Great Seal'[1] to the indentures. This refusal connects with their second means for exerting influence, that is, the claim to take cognizance of every grant and writ issued by the King. The great effects which this claim has produced, since from it flows the modern doctrine that all writings proceeding from the King need the counter-signature of a Minister, make it allowable to trace its history with some minuteness.

From the earliest times of the Norman

---

[1] Vide on subject of 'The Seals,' Proceedings of Privy Council, vi. Preface, pp. cxli to ccxix.

Monarchy, the King's will had been signified by 'writs' or letters, signed with the royal seal. No writing, it was early held, expressed the King's command unless accompanied by the impress of the seal. The necessity of some such guarantee for a document's genuineness was originally no legal fiction. For the frequent use Seals, why of 'tokens' is sufficient to show how great was required. the difficulty of warranting the authenticity of communications between man and man. Indeed this difficulty as naturally arises in a barbarous age as it is foreign to the ideas of those who are accustomed to the security of modern civilization. The King's 'Great Seal' was committed to the keeping of the Chancellor, and hence arose the necessity that this officer should have knowledge of all royal grants. This arrangement, which made the Chancellor a party to every grant, was primarily made for the King's convenience. He was extremely likely to grant away, without knowing it, his own rights; and it must have been an advantage to have a servant at his side to warn him of any danger to the prerogative. This convenience had, however, its price. The Chancellor who advised had the opportunity to remonstrate and cause delay, especially when the idea grew up, which was fostered by the Council no less than by the Parliament, that not only did every 'bill' (if this term may be used, in a wide sense, to describe every document signed by the

King), absolutely require the impress of the
Great Seal, but that the seal could not be legally
affixed without the Chancellor's intervention.
The plea in favour of this doctrine was the protection it gave to the Crown against the attacks
Kings' of fraud. Still most Kings felt it as a burthen,
endeavours
to evade and struggled against it in two ways. Either
this check. they maintained, that signature by smaller royal
seals, which, be it remarked, were retained in the
monarch's own possession, sufficed to give any
writing validity, or else they retained the ' Great
Seal' in their own keeping. Thus the Parliament remonstrated with Edward I, for issuing
writs relating to the Common Law, under the
Privy Seal, as also with Richard II in 1377.
Edward II, and Richard his imitator in all his
faults, each frequently retained the ' Great Seal '
in their own hands. Gradually however the cause
Privy Seal. of Law prevailed ; and though the Privy Seal became in some respects of acknowledged authority,
the prerogative gained but little, since the Privy
Seal passed into the hands of a regular officer.

Moreover the King's will was controlled in
another respect, through theories about the
'Seals.' The Chancellor made, originally, no
claim to do more than tender his advice about
grants, and did not presume to refuse to affix
the 'Great Seal.' But the circumstances of the
times suggested to him a plea for a further
extension of his authority. He owned, it may

be supposed, that he was bound to affix the 'Great Seal' at the King's command. But how was he to be assured that the King really did command? The assurance might come directly Verbal commands from the King's mouth, and in early times this held insuf- ficient. was, without doubt, considered enough. But, in many cases, direct verbal commands could not be obtained; and the Chancellor naturally demanded some more indubitable security that he was obeying the King's will than could be given by a mere message. The guarantee sought for was a letter signed with the King's Privy Seal. From asking for a warrant under the Privy Seal in cases where the King could not communicate his wishes by word of mouth, it was an easy step to pass to requiring it in every case whatever, and hence arose the doctrine, contested by the crown, and maintained by the lawyers, that no bill ought to be endorsed by the 'Great Seal' on a verbal warrant. In favour of this rule, the Chancellor could urge a plea, which had more weight than the legal fiction that it was impossible otherwise to know with certainty what really was the royal will. He might, with an appearance of justice, claim, for the sake of protection, some warrant which could be shown to others that in affixing the 'Great Seal' he had obeyed a royal mandate. Yet while this plea, and probably also the convenience to the Crown of throwing on its servants the responsibility for

its acts, reconciled the King to the restriction
placed on the free exercise of his will, the
restraint was one against which all monarchs
struggled, and even in the latter part of the
fifteenth century, Edward VI expressed indig-
nant surprise that his Chancellor did not deem
'Our own speech to you' sufficient warrant.

Attempts
to bring
all grants
under
Council's
notice.

Every accession to the influence of the Great
Law Officer was an addition to the Council's
power; and acts known to the Chancellor and
to the keeper of the Privy Seal must virtually
have come to the cognizance of the other
Ministers. But this indirect knowledge far
from satisfied the pretensions of the royal advisers. Various attempts were made to bring
all grants under the whole Council's observation. Thus in 1389,—the year, be it observed,
in which arose the dispute about the indentures
—it was enacted that every 'bill' (the word in-
cludes all writs and grants issued, as well as
petitions acceded to, by the king), should be endorsed by first the 'Signet,' secondly the 'Privy
Seal,' thirdly the 'Great Seal;' and, as though
this arrangement were not security enough that
the Council should be consulted, the ordinance of
the same year, before quoted, provides that no
grant to the detriment of the revenue should pass
without the advice of the Council. The accession
of the Lancastrian dynasty made no change in the
policy pursued by the Councillors. This policy

was now encouraged by Parliament, which passed, in 1406, a series of regulations more stringent than any before enforced[1]. Among other rules, it was enacted that all letters endorsed by the Chamberlain or Treasurer, and letters under the signet addressed by the Treasurer and the Keeper of the Privy Seal to the Chancellor should be endorsed by or written with the advice of the Council. The last and most important document which need be quoted on this subject is the ordinance of 1444[2]. Under the modest appearance of a series of formal rules about the presentation of petitions, it practically ensures that every grant of the Crown should, from the moment of its presentation as a petition to the time when it is formally issued as a royal writ, be under the notice of the King's Ministers.

The Lord of the Council and the petitioner who present a petition (bill) are each to subscribe it with their names. Petitions so signed are to be inspected by officials appointed for the purpose. These officers are commanded, according to the nature of the petition, to transmit it to the Common Law, to the King, &c. The petition, when signed by the King, is to be countersigned (to use a modern term) by Chamberlain or

Presentation of petitions.

---

[1] Rot. Parl. iii. 583–589. Proceedings of Privy Council, i. Preface lxii and pp. 296–298.

[2] Proceedings of Privy Council, vi. Preface clxxxvii and pp. 316–320. The date of this ordinance is a little uncertain.

Secretary, and when the bill is granted it is to be sent to the Secretary, who is to 'conceive letters upon it,' which are to be directed to the keeper of the Privy Seal, and from him sent, under the Privy Seal, to the Chancellor, to have the Great Seal affixed. 'If, however, the keeper of the Privy Seal thinks that the bills received by him under the signet contain matters of great weight, he is to refer them to the Council, who may refer them to the King again.'

Object of regulations.
These lengthy regulations in their main features resemble similar rules established in Henry VIII's reign, which, as regards royal patents, grants, &c., prevail at the present day. It is natural to enquire what exactly was the object with which they were formed. It sounds a satisfactory reply to say that they were meant to ensure the responsibility of Ministers. They assuredly had a tendency to produce this effect; and the fears of Richard's Council in 1389, lest Parliament should censure their acts, proves that the idea of ministerial responsibility was not entirely unknown to the statesmen of the fourteenth century. Nevertheless such an answer misleads, since it explains the conceptions of the fifteenth century by those of the eighteenth or nineteenth. These regulations were in no sense meant to shelter the Crown from danger and deprive it of powers, by substituting the rule of Ministers for that of the King. That

they were re-enacted by Henry VIII sufficiently shows that they did not necessarily curtail the prerogative. The ends which they were meant to attain were something different from ministerial responsibility, as that term is at present understood. These objects were mainly two-fold: first, to secure that the King should be in no manner cheated into consenting to grants which it was not his intention to make, or into conceding favours injurious to his revenue or his rights. To give him this protection, as many officials as possible were made responsible for every petition conceded; and thus a species of ministerial responsibility was established, but it was responsibility to the Crown, not to the Parliament: secondly, to secure that before any prayer was answered, the Council's advice should be taken. The anxiety to secure this is plainly seen in the reference back to the Council of all matters which appeared of weight. To this wish for knowledge of the royal acts, particular attention should be directed, since in it is seen the key to the whole history of mediæval Councils; for they are the embodiment of the feudal conception of government, in which the true limit to the royal power was the freely given advice of free Councillors. Yet while these were the only direct effects the Council proposed to attain, it was even then clear that such regulations had an immediate tendency to

(1) to protect the King,

(2) to secure Council being consulted.

control the prerogative; and hence the Councillors' humble though scarcely sincere protestations, that they proposed these rules (the words are their own, as far as a damaged MS. permits them to be given), 'humbly protesting they come before his said Grace only by way of advertisement, and none otherwise. For they in no wise think, nor have will to do, or .... anything, but that the King's good Grace do at all times as it shall please him, and use his power and will as it pertaineth to his royal estate.' These suggestions were brought before the King, agreed to, and after a few years, disregarded. Nevertheless they are important, since they mark the highest point to which the authority of the Council, as contrasted with that of the King, ever reached.

Every incident of the preceding sixty years had tended to increase the Council's might. The weakness of Richard II, his successor's doubtful claim to the throne, the long absences of Henry V, and still more the minority of his son, had all tended in the same direction. They had each, in different ways, made the Council the government of the state. Moreover the growth of Parliamentary power had led to the same result. During the minority at least, the Council was appointed by Parliament, which was therefore glad to strengthen a body which it did not as yet aspire to overshadow. Further, a change which had taken

Highest point of Council's authority.

Support of Parliament.

place in the Council's own constitution during the reign of Henry V tended at first to increase its authority. It assumed for the first time the title of the 'Privy Council,' instead of that of 'the Council.' The alteration of name must indicate a change in character; but its exact nature is nowhere clearly described. Many writers, indeed, speak of the difference between the 'Ordinary Council' and the 'Privy Council,' though they hardly point out wherein the distinction consisted. The difficulty of ascertaining its true nature is increased by the fact, that while the term Privy Council is not employed till the time of Henry VI, the expression 'Ordinary Council[1],' if found at all in the Council Records, appears but rarely, and would seem to have come into use through its employment by Hale. Reasonable doubts indeed may be entertained whether, prior to Henry VI, the 'Privy' and 'Ordinary' Council were in any sense distinct bodies. There existed, as has been seen, from a period certainly as early and probably earlier than Richard II's reign, a body consisting of regularly paid and sworn Councillors. These advisers were frequently assisted, as is testified by the ordinances, by the justices and judges. Originally those Councillors who regularly attended were perhaps scarcely distinguished

---

[1] Vide Palgrave, Essay on the King's Council, 20. Conf. Hale, Jurisdiction of Lords House of Parliament, pp. 4, 5.

from those advisers whom, like the judges, the King at times summoned. The minority of Henry VI, by flinging the whole government into the hands of the sworn Councillors, must have rendered the distinction between the habitual members of the Council and those, whether nobles, lawyers, or others, who were only occasionally summoned, much more marked. Hence, though the lines of demarcation between the two cannot be accurately drawn, the rise of a Privy Council from a general Council, which may be fairly called the Ordinary Council (though it admits of question whether the appellation itself is justified by any ancient records), is a well ascertained fact. That some distinction really arose about this period is an assumption not resting solely on the fact that the expression Privy Council is now first found, but confirmed by several incidents mentioned in the minutes. Of this kind are the special rules for securing the privacy of the Council's meetings, and the secrecy of its resolutions ; as for instance, in the Ordinance of 1426, which after alleging that ' great inconveniences ' had ensued from matters which had been ' spoken and treated in the Council having been published and discovered,' declares that ' from this time forward, no person of what condition or degree that he be, be suffered to abide in the Council, whiles matters of the said Council be treated therein, save only

Government thrown into its hands.

Formation of a more select Council.

those that be sworn unto the said Council, but if they be specially called thereto by authority of the said Council [1].' Such too is the account of a dispute between the Duke of Gloucester and the Cardinal Beaufort, in which there appears a marked contrast between a general and a more private Council [2]. It is, therefore, sufficiently apparent that under Henry VI a select Council was gradually arising from the midst of the general Council, that a change was taking place precisely analogous to the process by which, in a later age, the Privy Council itself gave birth to the Cabinet. Hence, from the concurrence of various causes, it resulted that the Council's authority had reached an extremely high pitch. The King was weak and incapable. The Council had long wielded the powers of the state, it had drawn close the bonds connecting its members together, and it thus stood, about the year 1444, prepared under cover of the regulations before referred to [3] gradually to seize, one by one, the prerogatives of the King. It is true that under the Tudors its powers, as against the people, were much greater than under the last of the Lancastrian dynasty. But this power had been purchased at the price of its independence, and it was as feeble against the Crown as it was mighty against every one else; whilst before

Era of Council's highest power, 1444.

---

[1] Proceedings of Privy Council, iii. 215. [2] Ibid. iv. 36.
[3] Vide p. 39, *ante.*

the Wars of the Roses commenced it towered
above every other constitutional authority.
At this point, therefore, the history of its encroachments on the Crown may pause, whilst
the reader turns to review the two other sides
of the Council's history during the Middle Ages:
first, its action as an administrative body; and,
secondly, its relation to the Law Courts.

It is inevitable that in writing the history of
any institution, attention should be primarily
directed to the different changes which it under-
goes; to its rise, its mutations of character, or
its decay. The point of view which the mind is
thus forced to occupy is apt to involve the writer
in error. He comes more and more to look
solely at the critical points in the history of his
subject, to fix his gaze on that which is exceptional, and overlook all that is ordinary; to
know how a given institution passed from one
stage of its existence to another, and not to
perceive what the institution truly was at any
stage whatever. No class of writers have been
more infected with this error than those who
have traced the history of the Privy Council;
for it is a history that necessitates the discussion
of antiquarian puzzles. Thus it has come to
pass, that whilst many have discussed what was
the Council's origin,—what the precise limits of
its jurisdiction,—whether its powers were legal
or illegal,—what was the distinction between

the Privy and the Ordinary Council, few have shown what was the daily existence of the Council during the Middle Ages. Yet a happy fortune places it within the historian's power, to bring before the imagination a picture of the Council's every-day life, which, if in many points indistinct and deficient, is as far as it goes correct. The means, and the only means, by which this picture can be obtained, is by study of the Privy Council minutes. In them the reader will find no historical theories, and, as the preceding sketch has shown, but little record of even important changes. As a compensation he has presented to his view, what may, with hardly an exaggeration, be called a daguerreotype of a feudal government. The picture has, it is true, the defects as well as the advantages of a photograph. It is colourless. Much is omitted which every one would fain see, and much recorded which, at first sight, could well be spared. Yet it has the great merit of truth, and it is soon felt not to lack interest. Did it come strictly within the scope of this essay, it might easily be shown that amidst dry accounts and wearisome lists of payments, these minutes contain traits of character, which can scarcely be surpassed by the descriptions of fiction. In them is recorded the manner in which the Percys were well nigh forced, by royal dishonesty, into the revolt which led to

Picture presented by Privy Council's minutes

their ruin. In them is given incontrovertible proof that the youth of the Fifth Henry was as warlike as his later years, and that the greatest English general of this age was no less active as an administrator than as a captain. In the same indubitable records is described the long struggle between Gloucester and Beaufort, in which the violence of the noble was again and again foiled by the craft of the priest. Beaufort himself stands depicted in the strangest colours as at once the greatest ecclesiastic, and the most grasping usurer of his day; who struggled with equal tenacity for his see and for his money; and exhibits all the contradictions of his nature in the petition containing in incongruous juxtaposition,—prayers that he might have good security for his loans[1], and might be allowed before he died to go a pilgrimage. Above all other characters of the period, towers forth by its nobility and grandeur that of Bedford. One sketch of whom afforded by these records, presents so lively a picture of himself and his times, that it may excuse a digression, which is after all a digression in name rather than in reality, since it gives an excellent view of the Council's manner of acting in moments of difficulty. A misunderstanding had arisen as to the extent of Bedford's power, and the Ministers came to remonstrate with him on

[1] Proceedings of Privy Council, iv. 235.

some undue claim to authority. Thereupon (the scene can scarcely be given in any other words than those of the minutes), 'it pleased his said lordship to say, that he had well heard and understood the matters above said, and he thanked them with all his heart that it lusted them to send to him for that cause, letting them wit that it was unto him one the greatest gladness to see the King, standing in his tenderness of age, to have so sad, so substantial, and so true a Council, and after it liked him to say, that he knoweth the King for his sovereign lord, and himself for his liegeman, and subject to him and to his laws . . . . And to put the said lords in more assurance, and comfort, as to the keeping and observance of the things above said, it liked my Lord of Bedford, of his own free will, to open the books of Evangile, lying in the Starred Chamber, and to swear by them, that he would truly observe, and keep, the things aforesaid. . . . And these words and many other gentle words he said so benignly and goodly, that tears sprung as well out of his eyes, as out of the eyes of all my said lords that were there present [1].'

While, however, the minutes of the Council contain many scenes of interest, it would be an absurd illusion to conceive that the plots of nobles and priests, or that great political acts of any kind, made up the daily occupation of

The Council as an administrative body.

---

[1] See Proceedings of Privy Council, iii. 231 to 243.

E

the rulers of the Middle Ages. The time of the Council was occupied, as that of every government must be, with an infinite number of trivial cases. It had at one moment to settle questions of policy; at another to provide funds, by which the administration could be carried on; at another to review minute accounts, to communicate with aliens or merchants, or to interfere for the preservation of the King's peace. It would be impossible, whatever were the length of this essay, to comprise the administrative functions of the Council under any definite number of heads. In modern days, legislative and judicial, administrative and political functions have been separated from each other to an extent which would have seemed unnatural to statesmen of the fifteenth century. Yet even after this separation has taken place, there exist bodies whose daily transactions could scarcely be brought under two or three distinct heads. Thus it would probably be impossible to form an exhaustive analysis of the occupations of a modern Cabinet. If so, much greater is the difficulty of analysing into clear divisions the transactions of that mediæval assembly which, in addition to the duties of a ministry, had to deal with matters which have since been relegated to the care either of law officers or of superintendents of police. Under these circumstances, the nearest approach to a sketch of the

Council's administrative action can be made by examining, first, what was the business on which it was actually engaged on particular days, selected pretty much by chance; and, secondly, by presenting an account on some special provinces, in which its power was called forth.

On the 20th August, 1389, the Council is engaged in negotiations with the Duke of Brittany about the restitution of the Earldom of Richmond. Their next business is to settle that Lord Stanley be Lord Lieutenant of Ireland, then to send an embassy to France, and to review the accounts of the Treasurer of Calais. Their deliberations, held in the King's presence, are concluded by arrangements with regard to certain pensions [1].

Look at the Council Board twelve years later. The meeting recorded was held some time in March or April, 1401. The business is even more than usually multifarious. The Council is occupied with the collection of the customs, a dispute between the Abbot and the towns' folks of Cirencester, and the despatch of J. Curzon, Esq., to Carlisle, that he may report the details of the last treaty with Scotland. They next arrange a list of Lords commissioned to enquire into the truth of accusations brought against certain malefactors in the county of Gloucester. They then accord an annual pension to the sons of Lords Salisbury and Oxford, till

[1] Proceedings of Privy Council, i. 128.

they attain their majority; give their attention
to the funds necessary for an embassy, which is
to conclude a marriage between the King's
daughter and the King of the Romans, and
resolve to take the royal pleasure on certain
points connected with the King's retinue.

One other example is sufficient. The assembly
is held during the reign of Henry V, May 27th,
1415. The first business entered on has reference
to an alliance with the Duke of Burgundy. The
Council then turns to money matters, and ar-
ranges to pawn the King's jewels, a mode of
raising money constantly recurred to by the
Crown in periods of distress. Various measures
are then devised for defending the kingdom.
The Chancellor is ordered to issue commissions
of array. Proclamations are to be made, ordering
a general election of beacons, and directions are
given about victualling the army and the fleet.
From civil the ministers direct their mind to
ecclesiastical matters, and enjoin the Bishops to
take measures to resist the malice of the Lollards.
Then follow matters of police. The Lord Mayor
is to be spoken to about the destruction of the
walls of the Friars Augustines, and to be cau-
tioned not to proceed with any demolitions in
the City without the advice of some persons
probably commissioners appointed by the Council. At the same time the Mayor is to be communicated with about the imprisonment of

certain workmen, who had been impressed in London for the royal service [1].

The minutes quoted exhibit the immense mass of business with which the Council was compelled to deal. The last quotation, with its references to means of raising money, to ecclesiastical matters, to the King's prerogative of impressment, and to the Council's interference with the privileges of the City, is deserving of especial notice.

It is impossible to give anything like a sketch, even in outline, of the Council's administrative labours. Four topics, however, from their importance, call for particular remark. *Four special provinces of Council's activity.*

I. *The Council's management of the finances.* Whoever looks down the long indices of the Council's Records, will observe that nearly every alternate minute has reference to some matter of accounts. Further inspection shows that the whole royal expenditure, whether the King's private expenses, or what would now be termed public finance, passed under the Council's review. Before the Council are laid budgets of the national expenditure; they are consulted on the best way of raising and of spending the revenue; and, while under monarchs such as Henry V, their accounts are strictly overlooked by the King (for even when occupied with the French war, Henry most carefully examined the statements submitted to him), during the minority of *1. Finance.*

[1] Proceedings of Privy Council, ii. 167.

Henry VI, and indeed during his whole reign, the Council regulated, under the guidance of ministers, such as Lord Cromwell, the finances of the country. Even though the fall of value in the precious metals, since the ages under consideration, be taken into account, the revenue and the expenditure sound small to modern ears. In 1421 the receipts were £55,743, and the expenditure, which however left several items unprovided for, £52,235. Yet no financial reformer need envy the moderate budget of a mediæval government. Small as the sums to be raised appear, they were not collected without extreme difficulty, and government payments were perpetually in arrear. The Percys were driven to revolt by ruin impending over them, through the King's tardiness in repaying their large loans. Nearly at the same time, the Prince of Wales was forced again and again to implore for supplies necessary to carry on the campaign in the Principality. Throughout the seventy years over which the records extend, the soldiers at Calais, on various occasions, satisfy their demands for pay by seizing the wools brought to the staple. The Council's resources under these difficulties are curious. One of the most ordinary was to pawn the royal jewels. When no more money could be acquired in this way, they employed, if Parliament could not be conveniently applied to for a subsidy, illegal methods for filling the Exchequer. Under Richard II certain persons were summoned before the Council without any assigned reason; and when they were brought thither, such sums were extorted from them as they were impelled to give, either by their loyalty or by their fears. Henry IV adopted an irregular but less oppressive plan; he persuaded a Council of nobles to supply him with funds; and requests for loans are to be found during the reign of every King. The Crown possessed however other ways of providing for its wants, than by extorting money. What it could not obtain in coin it took in kind. An instance has been already quoted, in which workmen were impressed [1]; and these exactions of labour were, if not considered strictly legal, yet submitted to, as a customary exercise of the royal prerogative. At any rate they were held to be justifiable, whenever the plea of the public defence could be urged. Thus on different occasions ships, and doubtless sailors, are impressed to convey armies across the channel. A mode of exacting money which was little likely to excite popular indignation, was to make special claims on resident aliens. An example of this occurs in 1415 [2], when the merchants of Florence, Venice, and Lucca, were informed that a loan was expected from them. They for a time re-

---

[1] Vide p. 53, *ante.*
[2] Proceedings of Privy Council, ii. 165.

sisted the demand, but yielded after undergoing imprisonment. These extortions, though suggested by the defenceless position of foreigners, may have appeared to be a reasonable repayment for the protection afforded them by the Crown, and lead naturally to the consideration of a second topic.

2. Aliens and trade,

II. *The Council's dealings with aliens and with trade.* It was to be expected that the Council should specially interfere with the affairs of aliens. Its power was, be it borne in mind, nothing but the King's prerogative exercised through his officers. In theory the prerogative had no limits. In practice it was limited, as regarded Englishmen, by the existence of certain rights on their side, which it is hardly an inaccuracy to say, were gained from the Crown by bargain. Rights so obtained could in no way affect foreigners. Those aliens, therefore, who settled in England, were both in theory and in fact, under the arbitrary rule of the monarch. Their rights, where they had any, were either the result of special concessions made to them by the King, or else of some particular treaty, contracted between the English Crown and the country to which they belonged. The position, therefore, in which aliens stood, during the Middle Ages, was not altogether unlike that occupied by foreigners, who at the present day take up their residence at Constantinople; since the rights of such persons depend on the conventions existing between their native country and the Sublime Porte. Treaties could be known only to the Council; and of their extent and validity, the King's advisers alone could be the judges. Let the situation of resident foreigners be understood, and their treatment by the Council, not only becomes intelligible, but affords a striking illustration of the fact, that the prerogative had no bounds, except where some established right came in to limit its exercise. From the position held by aliens arises the plea for exactions such as that before mentioned; from it, commands like those given to the Lombards in 1426, that they should write to their foreign correspondents, not in cyphers, but in language that all could understand; should export from the large ports only, and not enter the realm without the King's passport[1].

Besides issuing regulations of this description, the Council was bound to put into execution special rules about foreign merchants, made by Parliament. And here may be remarked, that there always have been, and still are, many particular powers, conferred on the Council by acts of the legislature. What these are could only be established by a survey of all the statutes, empowering the Council to act in special cases — a labour which would be as impossible to go

[1] Proceedings of Privy Council, i. 289.

through, as it would be vain to endeavour to express its results in an essay. The Council, however, appears to have been at liberty to relax the operation of statutes. A good example of authority given by Parliament, and of a statute's operation being suspended, is found in 1433, when 'it was accorded by the Lords of the King's Council, as towards merchant strangers, such as by the statute be bound to bring a certain sum for their merchandize to the bullion in the Tower of London, the Treasurer have power to grant them for the King's avail, such days of respite of bringing in their said sums to the bullion, as between them and him shall more be accorded[1].' No transactions give a better illustration of the footing on which aliens stood, and the Council's dealings with them, than does the history of the disputes between foreigners and Englishmen which were brought under the Council's notice. Thus a discussion arose in 1441, between Genoese merchants and the Lord Mayor, as to the payment of socage[2], in which the Council decided, that the Italians were to find security, and that the claim should be investigated. At the same time was brought before the King's advisers a complaint that English merchants were not fairly treated in 'Pruce, Hansze, and the Danske[3],' and an order was

Disputes between Englishmen and foreigners.

[1] Proceedings of Privy Council, iv. 145.
[2] Ibid. v. xci, and 169.   [3] Ibid. v. 170, 171, 178.

given that application should be made to these countries for redress. Other examples could be produced; but an account of this celebrated dispute, quoted from the Council Records, appropriately closes this branch of our subject; since it presents a picture of the Council's dealings with foreigners, and exhibits the way in which resident aliens were made, as it were, surety for the good treatment of Englishmen in the countries of which these foreigners were natives.

'The which [complaint] before them read, so seemed to the Lords [of the Council], that the complaint which the Englishmen made was of more likeliness true than else, and willing for so much as by the said complaint is shewed, that the said Englishmen were not treated, ruled, neither demeaned, in Pruce, Hansze, and the Danske, as they of these countries be treated here in England, and also that they be otherwise treated, ruled, demeaned in the said countries, than that the letters and seals of the Master of Pruce, remaining in the King's treasury, would ask or require, ... have therefore charged them of Pruce, &c., that time being before them, to write unto their countries and to the said Master and Governors of Pruce, &c., shewing unto them the said Englishmen's complaints, and desiring the wrongs to be redressed, and from henceforth to suffer Englishmen, merchants, to

use, and do in the said countries, as they have
done before this time, and as they ought to do;
for else the King and Lords will otherwise ordain,
in this behalf for the Prucieres being here, in
this land. For it was thought at that time, that
as they of England were ruled in the above said
countries, that they of the same, being now here
and repairing hither, should be ruled in semblable
wise [1].'

That aliens should, in an especial manner,
come under the Council's control, appears natural; but some surprise is excited by the
Government's interference with the general
course of trade. For the Council Records con-
clusively show that excessive intermeddling on
the part of the rulers with affairs of commerce,
is no new or modern evil. It is true, that the
Government meddled irregularly and with caprice; but its interference was of the kind of
which no ruler would now even dream. No
prerogative, for example, was more cherished,
and more constantly exercised by the Crown,
than the privilege of appointing certain places
as staples, i. e. as the sole towns whither it was
permitted to bring particular articles for sale.
The staple most frequently mentioned in the
Council's Records is Calais. The existence,
however, of numerous other similarly privileged
cities would, had every other monument perished,

Interference with course of trade.

---

[1] Proceedings of Privy Council, v. 170.

be kept in remembrance by the names Dunstable, Barnstable, &c. The custom of conferring the right of monoply on certain favoured localities, was so widely spread—a staple in Norway is referred to in the Council's Records—that it possibly was recommended by some real advantage. It may, in times of disorder, have facilitated the protection of traders. At any rate, it was by no means the most injurious restriction placed on trade. Innumerable statutes limited the freedom of commercial intercourse, as well between different parts of England, as between England and foreign countries. The operation of these acts was rendered more or less stringent, at the will of the Council. In 1422, license [1] was granted 'statutis non obstantibus' to the Earl of Westmoreland, to export to Middleburgh and Bruges five hundred sacks of wool, grown in Northumberland, Westmoreland, Cumberland, and the bishopric of Durham ; and in 1427 the merchants [2] of Newcastle were allowed to export from the said countries inferior wool whithersoever they pleased, without sending it to the staple at Calais. The Council possessed, in addition to the right of proclaiming staples and of regulating the effects of statutes, other modes of influencing trade. The government's practice of impressing labourers has been already referred to. The Council exercised the further

[1] Proceedings of Privy Council, iii. 115.   [2] Ibid. iii. 355.

privilege of erecting Guilds, as, for example, a corporation of London Parish Clerks in 1442. At other times it deprived corporate bodies of their privileges, for instance, it prohibited the craft of London Taylors from exercising the right of search amongst themselves, which had been conferred upon them, and ordered them to obey the Lord Mayor, according to the old usages and laws of London.

These details of the Council's dealings with trade have, in addition to their intrinsic interest, a peculiar value. Some of them throw light on rights which the Crown still exercises. The proclamations about trade in the fifteenth century, call to recollection the 'orders in Council' of the last French war, and proclamations about goods of war, still frequently put forth. The enforcement of statutes against aliens has still its parallel, whenever Alien Acts are put into operation. In the right of impressment was till lately seen a lingering vestige of the Crown's ancient claim to exact forced labour. Moreover, these extraordinary exertions of authority must be carefully noted, in order to understand how it was that the rule of the Tudors and Stuarts, while differing in essential repects from that of Henry VI, could nevertheless in many points preserve the form of a mediæval government.

3. The Church.   III. *The Council and the Church.* It was a

necessity that the Council should come frequently into contact with the ecclesiastical
powers. Still, on the whole, its minutes do not
contain so much reference to the Church as
might have reasonably been looked for. Allusions
indeed occur to the Council at Basle, and it is
clear that the Ministers of Henry VI watched
carefully the proceedings of that assembly.
The facts, however, recorded are of more interest
to the ecclesiastical historian, than to the annalist of the Privy Council's history. That the
contests between the English government and
the Court of Rome should have been but few,
during the earlier half of the fifteenth century,
is explained by the fact that the policy of the
house of Lancaster was to court the priestly
power, and that during part of Henry VI's
reign, Cardinal Beaufort's influence predominated
at the Council Board. Moreover, one great
cause of dispute—the question of the clergy's
right of appeal to Rome, had been decided in
favour of the Papal See. Some disputes, however, are recorded. The most important have
reference to the appointment of Bishops. In
these discussions the advantage remained, for
the most part, with the Papacy[1], though the
Council both maintained its right to make
ecclesiastical appointments, and, despite some

---

[1] Conf. Proceed. of Privy Council, iii. 210; iv. 76, 281.

signs[1] of subserviency to Papal influence, not only kept a jealous eye on the distribution of Bulls, but intervened in minor matters, where the Crown's interference would hardly have seemed to be necessary. At least it is surprising to find that a monk, who had procured the Pope's permission, to go to a 'harder order,' for the 'more quiet and peace of his soul, to the intent the more devoutly to serve and please Almighty God,' craved pardon of the Crown for ·having acted without its sanction; and that some nuns, desirous of enjoying the services of ' a good old Friar, a good preacher, a man of good conversation,' seek an order from the King to compel the Friars Minor to admit the said Friar to the priory of Rowner[2]. By far the most usual prayer from Churchmen was for exemptions from the Mortmain laws, and the Council's minutes are full of answers to this request.

Cases of heresy.

Before the Council came frequently cases of heresy or sorcery. The power exerted by the Crown, with regard to these matters, in a later age, makes it of interest to ascertain how the Council dealt with them under the Lancastrian dynasty. Allusions in the minutes to heretics or Lollards are not numerous. The charge given to the bishops[3] to suppress heresy has been alluded to, and rather suggests that the reason

---

[1] Proceedings of Privy Council, iii. 180.
[2] Ibid. vi. 66, 67, 68.   [3] Ibid. ii. 168.

why so few heretics were brought before the Councillors was that the bishops had power of themselves to deal with them. Thus, on the 2nd of January, 1406, the bishop of Lincoln is exhorted to bring before him certain persons accused of practising magic, sorcery, necromancery, &c., to the scandal of the Catholic faith[1]. On another occasion are brought before the Council persons charged with sorcery[2], who are dismissed after examination. In general the government seems to have been little disposed for active measures against heresy, unless false doctrine was combined with breaches of the peace; as, for example, when in 1431[3] a revolt took place in Oxfordshire, which had some connection with religious excitements, or when at Coventry[4] a friar openly aroused the people to attack the priesthood. In such cases the Council acted with vigour, though less as a defender of the faith than as protector of the King's peace.

and sorcery.

IV. *The Council as preserver of the peace.* The bare expression, 'the King's peace,' carries the mind back to a period when the phrase had an appropriateness which it has since lost; when public order, which now seems almost the natural condition of social life, was with difficulty secured, and when upheld was maintained rather as a royal privilege than as a national right.

4. The King's peace.

---

[1] Proceedings of Privy Council, i. 288. [2] Ibid. iv. 114.
[3] Ibid. iv. 107. [4] Ibid. vi. 40–45.

English monarchs, it is true, from the time of the Conquest, steadily opposed the right of the nobles to carry on private wars; but it is by no means clear that the nobility did not in early times think themselves at liberty to settle their own quarrels by force of arms. The claim, at any rate, to receive protection from the law, was looked upon in a light entirely different from that in which it is viewed in modern days, as is manifest from no fact more clearly than from the proclamation[1] by which Edward I put the whole clergy out of the law's protection, because they did not grant him a subsidy. To preserve therefore the public peace was as much the privilege as the duty of the Crown. This prerogative was, as a matter of course, exercised through the Council. The ordinary law courts also aimed at securing general tranquillity, but in cases where actual disturbances had arisen, the intervention of the executive government was at once more natural and more efficient than proceedings through the slow course of law, itself frequently impeded by the very violence which it was called upon to repress. Instances of the Council's interference abound. At one time Norwich[2], at another Northampton[3], at a third Coventry[4], are the scenes of armed violence,

---

[1] Stubbs, Const. Hist. ii. (Library ed.), 142.
[2] Proceedings of Privy Council, v. 15 & 290.
[3] Ibid. v. 191.   [4] Ibid. vi. 45.

and demand the attention of the royal Councillors. The assizes themselves are, on various
occasions, interrupted by the forces of neigh-
bouring nobles, and the Council are forced now
to stir up the sheriffs [1] to greater energy in the
maintenance of order; on other occasions, as
during the quarrel between the Earl of Devon
and Sir W. Bonville, to summon the offenders
before their bar [2]. The Council's interposition
was not, however, confined to cases of general
disturbance. In 1421 Sir James Berkeley [3] is
summoned to answer the charge of resisting, by
use of arms, the Countess of Warwick's entrance
into the manor of Wooton. At this point the
Council's character as preserver of the peace
merges in its other aspect as a law court, or (to
use modern expressions), its executive and
judicial functions become confused.

It is remarkable that while the Council's
minutes represent it as pre-eminently the executive
government, it is to its character as a law court
that attention has been almost exclusively
directed. The causes of this one-sided view of
the Council's position, which has been taken by
writers of repute, are to be found in the immense
extension [4] which its judicial powers acquired

[1] Proceedings of Privy Council, v. 35 ; or even the judges, *ibid.*
192.
[2] Ibid. v. 173, 174.   [3] Ibid. ii. 287.
[4] Conf. e. g. Palgrave, 'Authority of the King's Council,'
and Hallam's Middle Ages, &c.

under the Tudors, and in the prominence which this branch of its authority obtains in Parliamentary petitions. Yet the judicial aspect of the Council, though liable to cause error if viewed alone, is of first-rate importance.

The Council as a Law Court.

When the public peace was disturbed, the Council, as has been seen, took measures to preserve order. So far it pursued the course which would be taken by the governments of all ages. There is however a point where, in modern times, the action of the executive stops, since in no state of the present day is the government which suppresses a riot identified with the court which tries rioters. In the fifteenth century such an identification was to be found in the Council. Hence the Councillors went beyond the limits prescribed to the action of a modern government, and not only caused breaches of the peace to be repressed, but also summoned before their tribunal those by whom the peace had been broken. Thus, in the instances before referred to, of disturbances caused by Sir James Berkeley and Sir W. Bonville, the Council examined witnesses of the crimes committed. Again, the same body naturally called before it those who had stopped the course of justice. Whenever, in fact, either from defect of legal authority to give judgment, or from want of the might necessary to carry their decisions into effect, the law courts were likely to prove inefficient, then the Council stepped in, by summoning before it defendants and accusers. For example, some persons who, after invoking the arbitration of the Justices on a matter in dispute, refused to abide by their decision, are summarily brought before the Council[1]: the Countess of Stafford, on failure to appear, is condemned by default, and the quarrels of Ryman and Flete, of the Earl and Countess of Westmoreland, &c., are made subjects of judicial investigation.

Cases in which its judicial powers were employed.

A tribunal of this description was no doubt efficient, but its action was irregular and arbitrary, and from the time of Richard II to that of Henry VI its authority was met by the constant attacks of Parliament. This opposition has been before alluded to. It has been seen, that as early as Edward III the Commons remonstrated against the Council's judicial power. This authority had been exercised in two ways; first, by issuing special commissions of 'oyer and terminer;' secondly, by summoning accused persons. The first process had, after repeated remonstrances from Parliament, been abandoned, before Richard II ascended the throne. The second certainly survived, and even received extension.

Though Richard II's reign is the era when the Chancellor's separate equitable jurisdiction

---

[1] Proceedings of Privy Council, iii. 112.

Policy
of the
Commons.

first became firmly established, the Commons continue for a considerable period to combine in their remonstrances the names of the Council and of the Chancery. Indeed there is little reason to suppose that in the fifteenth century persons brought before the Council and those summoned to the presence of the Chancellor came before an essentially different court. In the first year of Henry IV, the Commons petition that all personal actions shall be tried at the common law, and not before the Council. At the beginning of the next reign a petition of a similar tendency is presented (3 Henry V). In the ninth year of Henry V the Parliament slightly changed their tactics. They attempted to put the Council under Parliamentary control, rather than to curtail its power. This endeavour failed, but in the earliest year of Henry VI's reign the attack is renewed. The proposed enactment of 1422 throws some light on the Parliament's views. It is in substance that ' No

Proposed
enactment
of 1422.

one shall be compelled to answer before the Chancellor, or the Council, or elsewhere, concerning any matter where remedy was given at common law, and that no writ of subpœna should issue commanding any one to appear in Council, or Chancery, until the plaintiff should have exhibited his bill, which shall be examined and approved by the Justices of the one bench or the other, that the complainant of the matter or grievances in the said bill cannot have action or remedy at the common law in any manner[1].'

This petition, like all others of the same tenor, was not suffered by the Crown to pass into a statute. It is remarkable, as being the last protest made for some ages against the Council's power. Thirty years later the feelings of the Commons appear to have changed, and the Act (31 Hen. VI) passed in alarm at Cade's rebellion, enhances the authority of the Council. The failure of the Commons' efforts, and their apparent alteration of policy need explanation. This is easily discovered, by examining what their opposition to the Council's judicial power really meant. They had various reasons for viewing with jealousy the habit of summoning persons before the King's Ministers. One doubtless was that such summonses were made instruments of extortion. Another was the hostility with which they looked on the decision by the arbitrary will of the King of questions which should have been decided by the immutable rules of regular law. With this feeling was combined a somewhat different sentiment, of dislike to the introduction of the civil law. The Parliament consisted, to a great extent, of common law lawyers, and was animated by their professional feelings. The struggle therefore carried on by the Commons was directed

[1] See Palgrave, 'Authority of the King's Council,' pp. 50–52.

as much against the equitable jurisdiction of Chancery, as against the arbitrary exercise of the prerogative. From this source the failure of their efforts. The Chancellor's equitable jurisdiction, though liable to abuse, conferred considerable real benefits, especially as the ordinary Judges were too much tied down by technical rules. Thus, by assailing an institution which was of true value, the Commons weakened the force of their attacks on arbitrary exercises of authority which were an indubitable evil. Moreover the circumstances of the times had gradually changed before the Commons relaxed the vigour of their attacks. The Court of Chancery had gradually come to act, though not on the same principles as those of the common law courts, yet on rules as fixed. Meanwhile the Council's judicial authority had, to judge by the minutes of Henry VI's reign, been exerted chiefly in cases where from the might of the offenders the courts really were powerless to enforce justice. Everyone also must have felt that the perils of the age which saw the Wars of the Roses, were rather the lawlessness of the nobles than the tyranny of the Crown.

Were the Council's judicial powers legal? It is, indeed, a question agitated by writers of great eminence, whether or not the judicial power of the Council was legal. The inquiry has a real meaning, when made concerning the authority exercised by the Council under the

Tudors; but it may not be presumptuous to suggest, that made with reference to the Council of the fifteenth century, the question is futile. Judged of by our conceptions of law, the authority of the Council must be pronounced arbitrary. Were, however, these conceptions entertained by any statesman in the age of Richard II, or of Henry VI? It may, it is true, be urged that the Commons attacked the use of the Council's power. This is true, but it must be remembered that the Commons themselves were ready to leave the Council a field of action, wherever men needed to be coerced, whose might rose above that of the law.

Though the lawlessness of the Middle Ages has become a trite expression, few possibly have formed any adequate idea of what the lawlessness in reality was. The difficulty of doing so is increased by the fact, that the amount of disorder actually existing varied greatly under every different king. William I and his vigorous successor administered an efficient, if rough-handed species of justice; moreover, the feudal system itself, when at its best, set some bounds to disorder. Gradually the system gave way. Under Henry VI anarchy had reached its height. The Wars of the Roses were a struggle, devoid of any principle on the part either of the conquerors, or of the conquered. Nevertheless, they fill an important place in

Lawless-ness under feudal system.

history, since they are neither more nor less than the break-down of the feudal system. The following passage, quoted from an ordinance, gives a glimpse into the general confusion existing at the outbreak of the Civil Wars.

'In eschewing of divers riots, excesses, misgovernance, and disobedience against the King's Estate, and for the peaceable governance of his laws, and in example giving of restful rule and good governance to all his subjects, it is advised by the said Lords of the Council, determined, and ordained, that no Lord, of what estate, degree or condition that he be of, wittingly receive, cherish, hold in household, nor maintain pilours, robbers, oppressors of the people, manslayers, felons, outlaws, ravishers of women, against the law, or any other open misdoer, so that the parties grieved by them shall not dare more pursue against them lawfully, because of such support of his Lordship; and also, that neither by colour, or occasion of feofment, nor otherwise, my said Lords shall take no men's cause or quarrel in maintenance, or conceive against any judge, or officer, indignation, or displeasure, for doing his office in form of law, nor lette by words, writings, or elsewise, the King's common law to have its course [1].'

This ordinance bears on its face the voucher for the truth of the evils denounced; and it is

[1] Proceedings of Privy Council, iii. 217.

easy to understand, that in a state of society where noble lords opposed the Justices, and 'maintained and cherished' robbers, pillagers, and ravishers of women, the people turned with hope to the King and his Council, who professed at least to prefer the cause of the poor, and by means, arbitrary it might be, but yet efficacious, gave justice in those numerous cases where there was 'too great might on the one side, and too great unmight on the other.'

PART III.

HENRY VI TO WILLIAM IV.

Gap in the Council's history. IN the records of the Privy Council occurs a long blank. From 1460 to 1520 there exists no memorials of the government's daily transactions. The effect produced by this gap is to place side by side two most different eras of English history. The weakness of the last Lancastrian is brought into immediate neighbourhood and stands in striking contrast with the might of the most powerful of the Tudors. At the date when the records fall short, the Crown had fallen to its lowest depth of degradation. The King was imbecile. A claimant to the throne had appeared, who had already wielded the power of royalty, and seemed about to demand its title. Throughout the land reigned that worst form of anarchy, in which the leaders of disorder are nobles. The age was one in which the nobility were everything. The barons had long defied the royal authority. They neglected summonses to Parliament. The great Councils, then almost yearly held, were rather assemblies of armed nobles than either Parliaments or the meetings of the King's advisers. In 1520 all is changed;

a King is on the throne whose title is too good
to be disputed, and whose power is too great
to allow even a doubtful title to be questioned.
The nobles who had defied the just rights of
Henry VI dared not oppose the most arbitrary
decrees of Henry VIII. The change was no
mere alteration of men. It had happened often
enough before that a vigorous monarch had
succeeded to a feeble ruler; an Edward I re-
gained the authority lost by a Henry III. Now,
however, it was a change, not of persons but of
circumstances. In other ages the influence
of particular kings had been increased. Now
the power of the Crown itself had arisen. To
trace the causes of this revolution belongs to
general history. The change itself may be Changed
summed up in the statement, that the feudal state of
nobility had been broken to pieces. It is nation.
scarcely a paradox to assert, that from the
weakness of the sixth Henry arose the strength
of the eighth. No astuteness of policy could have
brought the nobles to ruin so complete as the
destruction to which they were hurried by their
own violence. In wars where different principles
are opposed to each other it sometimes happens
that zeal for a great cause will lead men to overlook private animosities. When war is carried on
to obtain nothing but the objects of ambition, the
enthusiasm which finds no scope for its exercise
in the promotion of a noble end, degenerates into

bitter hatred of opponents. Such a contest was the War of the Roses. No principle animated the two sides. No plea of public good was even put forward. Whether any man was a Yorkist or a Lancastrian depended solely on his connections or his interests. Yet just because no principle was at stake the contending factions were divided from each other by the most intense feelings of hatred. Neither side was content with bare victory. The triumph of the battle consisted in the subsequent destruction of distinguished adversaries. The execution of the Duke of York and the murder of Henry's youthful son mark the spirit of the contest. Hence, when the war closed, scarcely one noble family existed of which members had not fallen by the sword or by the axe. It wanted but the cunning of Richard III, and the crafty policy of Henry VII to complete the work which the aristocracy had themselves begun, and when Henry VIII mounted the throne he found a nobility more broken in spirit than it has fallen to the lot of any other English monarch to govern. Their thorough depression is proved by the fact, that they did not resume a tone of independence till the reign of Charles I. For whatever opposition was made to the Crown's arbitrary acts during the rule of the Tudors proceeded from the Commonalty, and not from the Peerage of England.

The power of the Barons had in former ages curbed the will of the King. In later times the Commons curtailed the prerogative. In the age of Henry VIII the authority of the nobles had fallen, and the influence of the Commons, as far as it existed, supported the might of the Crown. 'Otium divos rogat' has, at different periods, expressed the wishes of a whole people. It represents the prayer of the English Commons when Henry VII seized the throne. The petition was fully answered, for civil wars of half a century were followed by a hundred and fifty years of almost unbroken tranquillity. Unlimited, however, as was the power of the Tudors' government, it appears at first sight difficult to see in what its strength consisted. The modern notion of a strong government is one disposing of a large army. In France, before the age of Henry or Elizabeth, the rulers had possessed themselves of this instrument of power. In England a standing force was unknown. A few yeomen of the guard added something to the dignity, but nothing to the might of the Crown. Henry VIII did not even make an effort to obtain a regular army. So foreign was a body of trained soldiers to English notions, that till the age of the Commonwealth, no permanent army existed, and its existence was first acquiesced in by the nation, after the revolution of 1688. What then was the foundation on

Foundation of the power of the Tudors.

which the power of the Tudors rested? The
answer belongs directly to the subject of this
essay. For, from the accession of Henry VII
to the sixteenth year of Charles I, the history
of the Council is the history of the regal power.
The century and a half—1485 to 1640—which
opens with the victory of Bosworth and closes
with the meeting of the Long Parliament, is a
period of manifold changes. During its course,
the Church was revolutionised, the crowns of
England and Scotland were united on one head,
the power of the Parliament first counterbalanced,
and at last overtopped the might of the prerogative. Nevertheless, to any one who reviews
the history of the Council, these hundred and
fifty years present a certain semblance of unity.
They might be described as the age of 'government by Councils,' and exhibit, in the strongest
colours, the merits and defects of a system nearly
as different from the rule of Henry V as from
the ministerial government of Victoria.

Constitu-
tion of
Council.

In 1553, King Edward VI drew up a series of
regulations for his Council, which, says Bishop
Burnet, ' he seems to have considered much, and
been well pleased with.' The picture given does
not, in every detail, apply to the Council as it
existed under either Edward's predecessors or
his successors. In the main, however, it gives the
best conception which can be obtained of what
the Council was during the hundred and fifty

years of its highest authority; and, when combined with other information, proves that the
constitution of that body had changed considerably since 1460. The Council of 1553 consisted Regula-
of forty persons[1]. They were divided into five tions of 1553.
commissions, or (to use a modern term) com-
mittees[2].

1. A committee for hearing those suits which Commit-
were wont to be brought to the whole board. tees of Council.
This commission was to hear suits, to answer
the parties, to make certificate what suits they
think meet to be granted, &c. Also to despatch all

---

[1] Burnet's Reformation (Clarendon Press ed., 1865), vol. ii.
pp. 357, 358; vol. v. pp. 117–120.

[2] List of Councillors :—

1. The Bishop of Canterbury.	20. Mr. Secretary Petre.
2. The Bishop of Ely, Lord Chancellor.	21. Mr. Secretary Cecil.
	22. Sir Philip Hobbey.
3. The Lord Treasurer.	23. Sir Robert Bowes.
4. The Duke of Northumberland.	24. Sir John Gage.
	25. Sir John Mason.
5. The Lord Privy-Seal.	26. Mr. Ralph Sadler.
6. The Duke of Suffolk.	27. Sir John Baker.
7. The Marquis of Northampton.	28. Judge Broomley.
	29. Judge Montague.
8. The Earl of Shrewsbury.	30. Mr. Wotton.
9. The Earl of Westmorland.	31. Mr. North.
10. The Earl of Huntington.	32. The Bishop of London.
11. The Earl of Pembrook.	33. The Bishop of Norwich.
12. The Viscount Hereford.	
13. The Lord Admiral.	34. Sir Thomas Worth.
14. The Lord Chamberlain.	35. Sir Richard Cotton.
15. The Lord Cobham.	36. Sir Walter Mildway,
16. The Lord Rich.	37. Mr. Sollicitor.
17. Mr. Comptroller.	38. Mr. Gornold.
18. Mr. Treasurer.	39. Mr. Cook.
19. Mr. Vice-Chamberlain.	40. Mr. Lucas.

matters of justice, and to send to the common courts those suits that be for them.

2. A committee for the calling of forfeits done against the laws, and for punishing the breakers of proclamations that now stand in force.

3. A committee for the state.

4. A committee to look to the state of all the courts, especially of the new erected courts, as the Augmentations, the first fruits, and tithes, and the wards, &c.

5. A committee for the bulwarks.

This distribution of official duties is followed by various regulations. They are minute, but do not differ essentially from those established in former reigns. Their main peculiarity is the care taken that every matter should be brought under the royal notice, and that the Secretaries should be a channel of communication between the Councillors and their master. The list of the Council, combined with the way in which the provinces of different committees are marked out, points to alterations in the assembly's internal constitution. The Council in 1553 forms a much larger body than it usually did in preceding centuries. Great prominence is given to the Secretaries, officials who at an earlier date are rarely mentioned. Their history throws light on the gradual alteration in the Council's position, and is moreover deserving of especial attention from its

The Secretaries.

connection with the growth of the modern Cabinet[1]. Originally their situation had little dignity or importance. The Secretary (for in the earliest ages there was only one) was, what his name suggests, merely the King's clerk, an appellation by which, until the reign of Henry III, he was frequently known. In rank, pay, and estimation, he stood on a level with the clerk of the kitchen, the chaplain, and the surgeon. He possessed no political influence, unless, as at times happened, he was one of the Council. The number of Secretaries was, after some changes, increased to two, and by almost imperceptible degrees, the dignity of the office increased. Thus, Beckington, who held the Secretaryship under Henry VI, was a diplomatist of considerable reputation. Under Edward IV various bills and warrants are made to pass through the Secretaries' hands. Nevertheless the same rank is assigned them in 1482 as at an earlier date. From 1485 a change is noticeable. The men who filled the Secretaryship are persons of importance. Dr. R. Fox, who served Henry VII as Secretary, became Bishop of Exeter. Dr. King, his successor, was considered a fitting person to sign a treaty with Portugal. During Henry VIII's reign, the Secretaryship is occupied by men such as Cromwell, and from this period the Secretaries take rank with a

---

[1] Proceedings of Privy Council, vi. Preface.

baron of the realm, always are members of the
Council, and at last by 31 Hen. VIII are made
so *ex officio*. They had then gained an important
position, which they have never lost, and it
needed but one step more for them to pass from
mere Secretaries into Secretaries of State.

The ordin-
ary Privy
Council-
lors.

Another peculiarity in Edward's Council is
the admission of persons, such as the two
Judges, who do not belong to the Committee
for the State. This is the sign of an alteration
which had taken place. In the reign of Henry
VIII appear, for the first time, some so-called
'ordinary' Councillors, of whom some never
and others rarely signed documents which bear
the signature of Privy Councillors. From these
facts may be inferred, that from Henry VIII's
reign the Councillors were divided into Privy
Councillors and Ordinary Councillors; or, what
perhaps is more probable, that while all called
to the Council Board were of equal rank, many
Councillors were, as a matter of course, not
consulted on questions of general policy, but
acted merely as a member of particular commissions mostly of a judicial character. The
existence of such Councillors is of importance,
because it explains some points in the late
history of the Council, and shows what was one
of the steps by which originated the custom of
appointing Privy Councillors, who hold the
title without performing the duties of the office.

The Council's internal changes depended The Council's Position. entirely on the great and important alterations which had taken place in its position. The mere catalogue of Councillors tells of a revolution since the day when all the important offices of government had been in the hands of nobles. Of the forty persons making up the whole Council, twenty-two are commoners, whilst in the most important of the committees, that 'for the State,' out of twenty persons seven are commoners, two bishops, and eleven noblemen. In the other commissions the majority is formed of untitled persons. This was no novelty of Edward VI's reign. In 1536 the Yorkshire rebels complained that the Council was filled by men of humble birth. The King's reply scarcely denies the charge, but palliates it by the assertion, that whilst there were then in the Council 'many nobles of birth and condition [1],' at the King's accession there had been among the royal advisers, 'of the Temporalty but two worthy calling noble, ... others, as the lord Marney and Darcey, but scant well born gentlemen, and yet of no great lands ; the rest were lawyers and priests, save two bishops.' The Council had entirely changed its position with reference to the crown. It had ceased to be a Dependence on Crown check on the King's will, and sunk into a body of officials. No change of outward form had

[1] Proceedings of Privy Council, vii. Preface, iii, iv.

been necessary to work this alteration. Henry
VII exercised no right which did not in theory
belong to Richard II. None the less, he and his
successor carried out a revolution. The independence of the Council had rested on the
presence of men who could not easily be
removed. The introduction of numerous commoners changed the nature of the whole body.
The nobles might retain their hereditary offices,
but these offices themselves had ceased to be
important. In nearly every one of them a
by depres-
sion of
nobles
deputy performed the duties, and possessed the
real influence of the place, whilst the nominal
superior added by his presence dignity to the
assembly, without himself possessing weight or
authority. England was governed, not through
peers of ancient lineage, but through the Cromwells, the Sadlers, the Petres, and the Cecils,
who constitute the glory of the Tudors' rule.
The promotion of such men was a national
blessing; but it increased immensely the power
of the Crown, by undermining the independence
of the Council.

Another cause tended at the same time
towards the same result. The presence of ecclesiastical dignitaries had at other times been a
source of strength to the Council. In the reigns
of Henry VII, of his son, or grandson, churchmen continue to advise the Crown. They give,
however, to the assembly in which they sit no

element of vigour. Even before the Reformation, bishops had ceased to look towards Rome, as the fountain of honour. Wolsey served too well his King, not his Church. With the Reformation the bishops became the dependents of the Crown. The Church must have sunk low, when a Queen and depression of Church. could write to a bishop, struggling to protect his see from spoliation:—

'Proud Prelate. You know what you were when I made you what you are. If you do not immediately comply with my request, by God, I will unfrock you. Elizabeth.'

Many signs of the state of dependence into which the Council had fallen, can be given. On many important occasions it was not consulted. Wolsey knew nothing of Dr. Wright's mission to Rome, in 1527; and, when Henry contemplated an interview with James V, in 1541, he communicated his intention to no one, except the Chancellor, whose aid was necessary in drawing up passports[1]. The rise of the Secretaries, to which reference has already been made, was at once a sign and a cause of the Council's declining independence. These functionaries came into immediate communication with the King. They were completely under his direction, and were employed in preference to other Councillors, because the absence of official dignity secured their obedience, whilst their

[1] Proceedings of Privy Council, vii. Preface, xii, note 1.

knowledge of business made them good servants.

Posthumous influence of Henry VIII.

The Council's acts paint its character. That the ministers were slow to oppose Henry, during his lifetime, is intelligible. But the influence of his commands after his death is more extraordinary. His will ordered that 'his executors should make good all he had promised, in any manner of way.' In obedience to this injunction, the Councillors made immense distributions of lands and titles. Here the calls of duty and of self-interest coincided. In other transactions they paid less heed to the will of their deceased lord. It is, however, remarkable that their disobedience, no less than their obedience, is marked by an impress of servility. Henry's design had been to place the Crown, as it were, in commission during his son's minority. A body called executors [1] were to stand in the place of the King, and the Privy Council was to assist them. With strange want of spirit the executors let Hertford (as Duke of Somerset) be raised to the regency; and, whilst they sunk into mere Councillors, rendered him independent of his Council. It seems as if the Councillors had so long been accustomed to occupy a subordinate position that they needed to create a master when one did not exist. Their behaviour stands in remarkable contrast with the course pursued

[1] Hallam, Const. Hist. (8th ed.) i. pp. 38, 39.

by the Council of Henry VI. At his accession there existed a Council of regency. Then also a nobleman wished to occupy the position of royalty. The claims of Bedford, or of Gloucester, to hold the royal power were greater than any possessed by Edward's uncle. Nevertheless their pretensions were manfully withstood, and a scene, already recounted, shows the vigour with which ministers of the fifteenth century dared confront demands to which the Councillors of the sixteenth offered no opposition. One more example of the Council's dependence suffices. The advisers of Henry VI, under forms of deep respect, frequently offered recommendations which were obviously meant to be commands. The ministers of Edward VI were, by the time he had reached the age of seventeen, already his servants. The whole tone of the regulations which he drew up proves this. In such orders as that ' on Saturday morning they shall present this collection (of business done in the week), and know the King's pleasure upon such things as they have concluded, and also upon private suits[1],' that ' if there arise such matter of weight as it shall please the King's Majesty to be himself at the debating of, then warning shall be given, whereby the more shall be at the debating of it:' or, again, that 'all warrants for reward,

Regulations of EdwardVI.

[1] Burnet's Reformation (Clarendon Press edition, 1865), vol. v. p. 122.

above forty pounds, and for his business and affairs above a hundred pounds, pass not but under His Majesty's signature:' breathes the spirit of one who felt himself to be the real head of the state.

Increase of Council's power as regards people

As the Council's independence lessened its powers increased. This was to be expected: since from the moment that the Councillors became thoroughly dependent on the Crown it was the King's interest to enlarge the field of their authority. For, while it had always been the royal desire to enlarge the extent and force of the Council's powers, it became tenfold more the King's interest to do so as his advisers sunk into his ministers. But what had been the occasional wish and endeavour of other monarchs became the fixed policy of the Tudors. Whenever it could be done, parts of the kingdom were brought under the Council's direct

by (1) subjection of special places to Council's government;

control. Poyning's Act of 1494 placed the Irish Parliament under its rule, and (though the circumstance is of no weight in itself) it is a curious sign of the prevailing policy that during Henry VII's reign Jersey and Guernsey were brought beneath the direct government of the Council. At the same time every opportunity was taken to erect special Councils for the government of different parts of England. Though they were founded at various periods, and under different monarchs, their formation was carried out so consistently, that in 1640 the bodies existing under the names of Councils of the North, of Wales, &c., ruled, it is said, over a third of England. These tribunals were formed on the model of the Privy Council, and were to some extent dependent on it. Their nature can be understood only by following in detail those steps by which the Council's powers were extended.

Among the regulations of 1553, is one calculated to arrest attention, to the effect that 'there be a commission for the calling of forfeits done against the laws, and for the punishing of offenders against proclamations which now stand in force.' The point which requires explanation is the nature of proclamations. At all times it has (2) power been the natural prerogative of royalty to issue of procla-mations. proclamations of the royal will, of the state of the law, of warning to those likely to commit offences, or of encouragement to arrest those who had offended. These proclamations are regarded as solemn expressions of the King's will, and are always put forth 'with the advice of the Council.' Their exact force is a matter which even now cannot precisely be decided, since it labours under the uncertainty affecting all questions bearing on the limits of the prerogative. The best established opinion is, that while a proclamation cannot make a law, it can add force to a law already made; that (to use the

words of judges [1] living in the reign of Mary)
'the King may make a proclamation *quoad
terrorum populi*, to put them in fear of his displeasure, but not to impose any fine, forfeiture,
or imprisonment ; for no proclamation can make
a new law, but only confirm and ratify an
ancient one.' Though this was the view of the
lawyers, it was not the opinion held by the
Tudors. Their constant aim was to give proclamations the force of laws, and thus to render
the King's Council a legislative body. Had the
endeavour succeeded, the Council would have
occupied the position of a French Parliament ;
a body to which, both in origin and history, it
bore a close resemblance. The attempt was for
a moment crowned with success. In 1539,
Henry VIII [2] obtained from the most servile
of Parliaments, that 'proclamations made by
the King's Highness, with the advice of his
honourable Council, should be obeyed and kept,
as though they were made by Act of Parliament.'
The hand of a vigorous ruler was needed to wield
power so immense. The regency who succeeded
Henry were not equal to the task, and the act
was repealed [3]. Though, however, no further
attempt was made to transfer the legislative
functions of Parliament directly to the Council,
proclamations were nevertheless treated much

---

[1] Conf. Hallam's Const. Hist. (8th ed.) i. 337.
[2] 31 Hen. VIII. cap. 8.   [3] 1 Edward VI. cap. 12. s. 4.

as laws. Under Edward VI many ecclesiastical changes were first promulgated by proclamation, and afterwards sanctioned by Parliament. In 1549, the justices were ordered by the same means to arrest tellers of vain forged tales, and commit them to the galleys, there to row during the royal pleasure. In the reigns of Mary and Elizabeth, proclamations were perpetually issued. By them Anabaptists were banished, the culture of woad forbidden, and the further increase of London—a constant object of royal solicitude—prohibited. It was, moreover, one of the Star Chamber's special cares to enforce the observation of proclamations 'not yet made into statutes.'

The weight given to the Council's edicts was not the sole or main extension of its sway. The great aim of royal policy was to place the law courts under its influence; various means were employed to effect this object. New Courts were erected, such as the High Commission Court, the Court of Requests, the 'various new courts' (mentioned in the regulations of 1553), which to a great extent consisted of Councillors, and were all under the supervision of the Council. All these instruments of despotism sink into insignificance before the unbounded extension given to the Council's direct judicial authority, through the growth of the greatest institution produced by the

(3) Connexion of new Courts with Council.

(4) Extension of Council's judicial authority.

fifteenth and sixteenth centuries, the 'Court of Star Chamber[1].'

Some tribunals have grown to a height of power and influence, which endows them with a species of terrific grandeur. The Inquisition, the Revolutionary Committee of Public Safety, all those institutions by which might has for a period triumphed over right, together with the horror they cause, inspire a peculiar kind of interest. Every one abhors the great instrument of oppression; but every one feels a wish to know by what measures it was formed, what were the true sources of its strength, what the uses to which its might was applied. Among institutions at once powerful, hateful, and full of interest, the 'Court of Star Chamber' occupies no mean position. If its influence was less extended than the sway of the Inquisition; if its deeds lacked the bloody atrocity of the Revolutionary Courts; it combined system of secrecy in its acts which a Dominican might have admired, with a power of duration which might have inspired the authors of the Parisian tribunals with hopeless envy. For the Star Chamber was no temporary court. During a hundred and

Star Chamber.

---

[1] On the Star Chamber, vide:—

Hallam's Const. Hist. (8th ed.), i. 47–56, 233–236; ii. 30–35, 97, 98, 331.

Hudson, Collectanea Juridica, ii.

Palgrave, 'The Authority of the King's Council.'

fifty years its power penetrated into every branch of English life. No rank was exalted enough to defy its attacks, no insignificance sufficiently obscure to escape its notice. It terrified the men who had worsted the Armada; it overshadowed the dignity of the judicial bench; it summoned before its tribunal the Prynnes and the Cromwells, who at last proved its destroyers. It fell at length, but great was the fall thereof, and in its ruin was involved the downfall of the monarchy.

It is with something of astonishment that the *Its origin.* inquirer discovers that this august tribunal was merely the Council under another name; and that the court, whose overgrown power the patriots of 1640 cast to the ground, was the same body whose early encroachments had alarmed the parliamentary leaders under Edward III and Richard II. The process by which the judicial authority of the Council passed into the form of the Court of Star Chamber admits of some dispute, and is involved in no little obscurity. No one at the present day need feel ashamed to avow his ignorance, when he finds that even in the time of James I, when the Star Chamber was in full activity, men learned in the law could dispute no less as to its origin than as to its power; that a Plowden was pronounced in error, and that Hudson, the annalist and eulogist of the Court—for it possessed

fervent admirers—wrote his treatise principally
to dispel popular misconceptions which dimmed
the glory of his idol. The origin of the name is
itself shrouded in mystery. In the following
passage, Hudson unfolds at once the dignity of
the tribunal and the various derivations given
of its appellation :—

' Some think,' he writes, ' it is called a *Crimen
Stellionatus*, because it handleth such things,
and cases as are strange and unusual: some of
Stallen. I confess I am in that point a Platonist
in opinion, that *nomina naturá fiunt potiùs quam
vagá impositione ;* for assuredly Adam, before his
fall, was abundantly skilful in the nature of all
things; so that when God brought him all things
to name, he gave them names befitting their
natures..... *Camera Stellata* .... is most aptly
named; not because the Star Chamber, where the
Court is kept, is so adorned with stars gilded,
as some would have it; for surely the Chamber
is so adorned, because it is the seal of that Court,
..... and it was so fitly called, because the stars
have no light but what is cast upon them from
the sun, by reflection, being his representative
body; and as His Majesty himself was pleased
to say, when he sat there in his royal person,
representation must needs cease when the person
is present. So in the presence of his great
Majesty, the which is the sun of honour and glory,
the shining of those stars is put out, they not

having any power to pronounce any sentence in this court, for the judgment is the King's only[1].'

Modern historians have paid little attention to Hudson's courtly derivation, and have held it nearly certain that the account of the name which he rejects is the true one. The Court of Star Chamber is, as may be seen from the Records, the Council meeting in the 'Starred Chamber,' that is, in all probability, in a room the ceiling of which was adorned with stars. The history of the name has some importance, as an indication that the Star Chamber was the Council exercising judicial powers.

The exact growth of these powers it is not easy to trace. It is certain that from the time of Henry VII the Council or Star Chamber exercised a jurisdiction which, though bearing some resemblance to, greatly exceeded its exertions of authority at an earlier period. Two accounts are given of the rise of this judicial power. One refers it entirely to the statute 3 Henry VIII. The Act recites *intra alia* that, ' by unlawful maintenances, giving of liveries, signs and tokens, &c.; untrue demeanings of sheriffs in making of panels, and other untrue returns, by taking of money, by juries, by great riots, and unlawful assemblies, the policy and good rule of this realm is almost subdued,' and enacts 'that the Chancellor and Treasurer of England, and

Two theories about it.

_____
[1] Coll. Jur. ii. p. 8.

Keeper of the King's Privy Seal, or two of them, calling to them a Bishop, and a Temporal Lord of the King's Council, and the two Chief Justices of the King's Bench, and Common Place upon bill, or petition, against any person for any behaviour aforesaid, have authority to call before them, by writs or privy seal, the said misdoers, and others by whom the truth may be known, to examine . . . . and punish them, according to their demerits: after the form and effect of statutes thereof made, in like manner and form as they ought to be punished if they were thereof convict after the due order of the law.'

The opinion that to this statute is due the authority of the Star Chamber, is supported by much apparent evidence. The act which is recited in the preamble of 16 Car. I, cap. 10, is entitled 'an Act giving the Court of Star Chamber authority to punish divers misdemeanors[1].' To it Plowden referred the Court's origin. Despite, however, this weight of proof, another and a truer opinion has been maintained. Even in the days of James I, it was the doctrine of Ellesmere as stated by his admirer, Hudson[2], that the jurisdiction of the Star Chamber was merely the original jurisdiction of the King's Council. Historical examination confirms the justice of this view. That the powers given by the Act

---

[1] Statutes of the Realm, vol. ii. p. 509.
[2] Coll. Jur. ii. p. 51.

3 Henry VII, cap. 1, were exceeded, is stated in 16 Car. I, cap. 10, but in fact Henry's statute seems neither for good nor for bad to have exerted influence over the growth of the Star Chamber. The judges in that Court were the whole of the Council. The crimes punished by it consisted of many others than those enumerated in the Act. The penalties inflicted were not those assigned by statute.

It is, indeed, worth remark, that the offences enumerated in 3 Henry VII, cap. 1, e. g. acts of violence, resistance to justice, etc., belong exactly to that class of crimes which the Council had always claimed a right of suppressing. The conjecture may therefore be made, that the real scope of the Act was to regulate an authority which Parliament felt to be at once necessary and dangerous. The special Court thus established was in existence as late as 1529[1]. But soon afterwards its powers merged in the general authority of the Council, or Star Chamber. That this should have happened is less strange than it at first appears. All the business of the Council was transacted through committees, which were, as occasion required, differently modelled. The same persons sat, as may be seen by the regulations of 1553, on different commissions. Now the body constituted by 3 Henry VII, cap. 1, was essentially a

---

[1] Hallam, Const. Hist. (8th. ed.), i. p. 53.

committee of the Council, of which the members had no permanence. It was not unnatural that the functions of different committees should have been interchanged, and to some extent confused. Whatever may have been the cause of the change, it is at least well established, that towards the close of Henry VIII's reign the special commission created in 1488 no longer existed; that powers much wider than those conferred by statute were exercised by the Star Chamber; and that this Court, consisting mainly of Councillors, may without inaccuracy be identified with the Council.

Its constitution.   Hudson's treatise affords a means of forming a conception of the Council's constitution, powers, and action, as a law court. His sketch, which describes the Star Chamber with full accuracy as it flourished under James I, may not in every detail apply to it as it rose into greatness under the Tudors. The extent to which its character changed during the century cannot be ascertained. What alteration there was had probably tended to make it more of a law court and less of a Council; and a trace of this change is seen in the regulation of 1553, which creates a committee 'for hearing those suits which were wont to be sent to the whole board.' It stood, when Hudson wrote, in a position not altogether unlike that occupied by the Court of Chancery before the reign of Richard II, and it is possible (though the course of events under Charles I does not favour the supposition) that the Star Chamber, if its existence had not been cut short, might have ultimately become a Court as distinct from the Council as was the Chancery.

One reason why this never happened is to be found in a peculiar feature of the Star Chamber's constitution,—the frequent presidency of the King in person. The legal fiction that the King is present personally in all his courts, was here carried into act. In this respect, as in many others, the rule of the Tudors and Stuarts concealed revolution under the mask of restoration. For in the ancient 'Curia Regis' the King did actually preside, and the Star Chamber was in more points than one the 'Aula Regia' revived. In the royal presence 'no one,' writes Hudson, 'had any power to pronounce sentence; for the judgement is the King's only; but by way of advice the Councillors deliver their opinion, which he increaseth, or moderateth, at his royal pleasure.' The part taken by the King was no empty formality. On one occasion James presided for five days, 'seated on a chair high above the rest,' and terminated the case by pronouncing a sentence, of which, if the annalist is to be believed, the wisdom surpassed that of any judgment before uttered from an English tribunal.

Even when the King was absent, the Court

Presidency of King in person.

lacked nothing in dignity. Thrice a week in term time, and occasionally out of term time, it transacted business. At its head sat the Lord Chancellor. Councillors, as well as nobles not of the Council, were its judges. Its numbers, including many bishops, amounted at times to forty persons. In the reign of Elizabeth, peers, not Privy Councillors, desisted from attendance, and the number of the Court was lessened; though in later reigns as many as twenty-five Councillors sometimes attended. From the lowest to the highest, each man gave sentence in order, till the voice of the Lord Chancellor proclaimed the judgment of the Court[1].

Process.

It was not, however, the dignity of the judges which imparted to the Star Chamber its terrors, but rather its manner of procedure. The Council acted in one of two modes. The most summary was the proceeding *ore tenus*. On the reception of a charge by the Council—one grounded, it might be, on 'common report,' or on secret information, the accused person was privately arrested, and brought before the Council Board. There he was examined. If he confessed, or made admissions considered equi-

'Ore tenus.'

---

[1] It is a curious example of the Court's dignity, that after the day's labour it dined at the public expense, and that the cost of these banquets was, if the altered value of money be taken into account, considerable: e. g. in 1559, the ordinary charge of a dinner was £4 10s. to £5 9s.; in 1579, £8 to £10; in 1590, £17 to £18.

valent to a confession, he was condemned *ex ore suo*, and judgment was given against him. He knew neither his accuser nor the crime of which ho was accused, and he was subjected to an examination which, as even Hudson admits, was conducted with scanty fairness to the prisoner. He might, indeed, refuse either to confess or to answer any questions. If so, he was not condemned, but remanded to prison, that the Council might adopt another course.

This, the second mode of prosecution, was to By bill. proceed by bill. A bill of complaint was addressed to the Council, signed by a Councillor. When the bill was filed, or in some cases even before its filing, the accused was summoned by a writ of subpœna. On his appearance the defendant was bound to answer on oath the plaintiff's bill. If ho refused to make a reply, he was committed to prison; and, after some delay, his crime was treated as acknowledged. If he put in an answer, his case was not much better; ho was examined by the plaintiff on written interrogatories, a refusal to reply to any of which led to imprisonment of indefinite and sometimes life-long duration. After the plaintiff's examination, witnesses, whose character the accused was not allowed to shake, were privately examined. The cause was then ready for determination, and after, it might be, a long delay, sentence was given.

Penalties. The punishments which followed were of the most arbitrary character. Death was the only penalty the court dared not enforce. Fines, whipping, the stocks, the pillory, scourging, branding, were some among the long list of punishments. Sometimes a punishment appointed by statute, at times a penalty greater than any law warranted, was inflicted. Mere caprice would either lighten or aggravate the punishment. Abject submission was the best road to the Council's favour. Sometimes the crime itself suggested an appropriate recompense. There is a species of savage humour in the sentence that a man who objected on religious grounds to eat swine's flesh should be imprisoned, and fed on no meat but pork.

The Council's manner of proceeding was unlike that of other courts. Its punishments were as arbitrary as they were severe; it also exercised a power peculiar to itself of extorting confession by torture. Some, however, may imagine that powers so great were only occasionally exercised that exceptional exertions of authority were employed to meet exceptional crimes, and that gigantic force was put forth to crush gigantic evils. Some circumstances have given currency to such a notion. Everybody has heard of one or two great displays of the Council's powers, which have become matters of history. On the other hand, the cases where it interfered with the minor crimes, and the lesser concerns of life, have been for the most part forgotten. Yet no conception of the Star Chamber is more false than that which makes it a 'deus ex machina,' which intervened only when the lower courts of justice stood confronted by some criminal attempt with which they were too weak to deal. The sphere of the Council's jurisdiction was *Its sphere* unlimited. It is now no question of what it had *of action.* a right to do, but of what it did. And any one who examines the most certain facts of history will be convinced that from the accession of Henry VII till the meeting of the Long Parliament the Council interfered in all matters, small as well as great. It is, indeed, perhaps not generally known, that crimes of a very ordinary nature, such as would now come before a police magistrate, occupied the attention of the Star Chamber. Charges of robbery, murder, sheep stealing, theft; as, for example, of purloining the 'Queen's standish[1],' were investigated by Councillors. To give a complete analysis of the classes of offences punished by the Star Chamber is, from the nature of the case, impossible. All the misdemeanors which the statute 3 Hen. VII, cap. 1, enumerates, and many others, e. g. fraud, perjury, libel, disputes about civil rights, were brought before its bar. A few examples of offences actually punished may give

---

[1] Vide Jardine's Readings on Torture. Passim.

some idea of its jurisdiction. These are taken with equal propriety from the annals of the Council or the records of the Star Chamber. For it is impossible to draw any precise line between those offences which the Council punished, acting as a government, and those which it noticed in the character of a law court; and such a distinction, could it be made, would only mislead, for it would hide what is the characteristic feature of the period under review, the inseparable combination in the Council of political and judicial authority.

Whenever accusations of treason or sedition were preferred, the Council lent a ready ear to the accuser. Modern notions, however, of what is treasonable or seditious give a feeble conception of the meaning attached to these terms in the sixteenth century. Not acts alone, but slight expressions aroused the government's vigilance. Mr. Swynerton of Swyneshead was brought, in 1540, before the Council for exclaiming[1], 'O, Jesus, what a world this is, that so many men should die for one man's sake!' A parson was reported to have said, that 'he knew one or two persons who bore the King no good heart[2].' Forthwith his accusers were summoned, and strictly examined. It was not the insignificant alone who came as criminals before the

---

[1] Proceedings of Privy Council, vii. 31.
[2] Ibid. vii. 237.

Council. Sir Thomas Cheney was himself a Councillor, Warden of the Cinque Ports, and Treasurer of the King's Council. At the accusation, however, of his own son, he was examined by his fellow Councillors, on the charge of treason. The accusation fell to the ground, and the Council, arbitrary in its very justice, committed the son to the Tower 'for an example.'

Acts of this sort are rather proceedings of a despotic government than of a law court; but closely connected with them is the correction of a class of offences over which the judicial authority of 'the Council in the Star Chamber' was so exercised as to influence considerably a branch of modern law. The body which took notice of slight expressions was inevitably led to punish the crime of libel; and thus it is under shadow of the Star Chamber that originally grew up the laws affecting that offence. Hudson presents examples of the Star Chamber's proceedings with respect to libels [1]. The personation of Lord Lincoln on the stage, a coarse joke at one Holes were punished as libellous. Under the same offence was brought a letter (not published), sent to the Bishop of St. Asaph.

A tribunal as watchful as the Council was not likely to neglect the control of the press. The instrument for expressing public opinion was

Control of the Press.

[1] Coll. Jur. ii. 100.

rising into influence during the reign of Henry VIII, and the last volume of the Council's records gives proof of the jealousy with which the new power was viewed. The minutes contain lengthy inquiries concerning publications by Grafton. This printer was already before the Council, on the charge of publishing certain 'invectives,' when, by his own confession, he was found to have in his possession 'a certain seditious epistle, in the English tongue, by Melancthon[1].' He was committed to prison, and, with some other persons concerned in the publication of the pamphlet, let remain in the Fleet. These are some of the Council's early proceedings in its office of censor of the press. By degrees the Star Chamber became more and more of a regular censorship. In 1585[2], at the instigation of Whitgift, a proclamation was issued for the full regulation of the press; the whole printing trade was put under the superintendence of the Stationers' Company. Nothing was to be published which had not passed under the inspection of the Bishops. The Guild to which the control of the printing trade had been committed was empowered to search houses, in order to destroy books published in contravention of this ordinance, and to bring all offenders before the Council. From this time the supervision of

---

[1] Proceedings of Privy Council, vii. p. 106.
[2] Hallam's Const. Hist. (8th ed.), i. 239.

the press became a regular part of the Star
Chamber's duties. It, however, requires the less
notice because it has been rendered famous by
the treatment of Prynne. In the ordinance
regulating the press is seen a specimen of the
force given by the Council to proclamations.
This example alone would sufficiently prove the
truth of Hudson's assertion, that the Star Chamber
' stretched proclamations as far as Act of Parliament ever did.'

Besides asserting the right to act in almost
every case where a law court could interfere,
the King and his Councillors avowedly acted
in cases not examinable in other courts[2]. Of
these cases the breach of mere proclamations
was one, but it was only one out of a thou-
sand. For the Council had arrogated and exercised an authority not unlike that of a
censor. The spirit of the age during the sixteenth century was one of interference. In
affairs of religion, in questions of labour, in
matters of private life, the government inter-
meddled. It is probable that popular feeling
invited its intervention. The fact that government interference is an evil is now too well
established to need the confirmation of further
arguments. It is, however, by no means clear
that the baneful activity of rulers is generally unpopular. It was not so in the reign of
Henry VIII, or of his son. Among the latter's

Interference in private life.

remains[1] is found a curious illustration of the
sentiments of his time. In a paper on government he has given his notion of the measures
needed for the 'reformation of various abuses.'
The essay, which exhibits neither originality
nor talent, is valuable precisely because it gives
the very ordinary thoughts of an ordinary man,
and therefore represents the theories of the
age. From beginning to end it is an eulogy of a
'paternal government,' and alludes, with approval,
to encroachments on private rights, before which
the Cabinets of Vienna, or of St. Petersburg,
would now stand aghast. The young King had
learnt to think that this country could bear no
merchants to have more land than a hundred
pounds, no husbandman or farmer worth above a
hundred, or two hundred pounds, no labourer
much more than he spendeth[2]. The paper abounds
with theories of this description, accompanied
by the notion that a ruler's duty is to reduce
such speculative opinions to practice. When
these were the lessons inculcated on a youthful
monarch by his aged instructors, a part at least
of the nation must have looked with favour on
the interference of government in the affairs of
private life. The Council took full advantage
of the prevalent feeling. It interfered (to use a

[1] Vide Burnet's Reformation (Clarendon Press ed. 1865), vol.
v. p. 96.
[2] Ibid. p. 98.

modern phrase), 'in the interests of morality,' whenever either individuals or classes acted in a way which the law could not punish, but which moral feeling condemned. The minutes of the Star Chamber are crowded with punishments for attempts to commit crimes, for buying up commodities, and the like. In one instance is recorded the strange offence for which a woman is severely punished, of 'practising to have her husband whipped[1].' This punishment is rendered the more strange by the discovery that the injured husband was dead, and that his father performed the part of prosecutor. From the same desire to check any act which was thought to be 'contra bonos mores,' springs much of the Council's intervention in private disputes. Thus, when John Bulmer and his wife quarrelled, the Council at the wife's complaint[2] ordered the husband to make her an allowance of forty marks yearly, and let her dwell one year's time in her brother's house. Even at the end of the year Bulmer was not to be released from the payment of the allowance, unless 'he should resort to his wife, and use her after such a sort as it behoveth an honest man to use his wife.'

The Councillors at times composed the feuds of neighbours; and amidst more weighty matters, found time 'to set at one and make friends Sir J. Dene and T. Halcroft;' and on the same day

[1] Coll. Jur. ii. 108.
[2] Proceedings of Privy Council, vii. 321, 322.

to arrange the quarrels of David Vincent and R. Cecill, on which occasion the dispute was settled by giving Vincent 'an honest monition' for his fault, with the advice to the two foes 'to be friends.' No more than a few samples of the Council's system of interference can be given. Its measures to protect game, its summary orders, on one of the King's journeys, that corporations should pay their debts[1]; its proclamations, by which the people of York were induced to bring their grievances before the King, and the tyranny with which those who did complain were pun-ished[2], can be allowed but a passing allusion.

Control of Law Courts.

Some points, however, demand, from their importance, more particular notice. Among these stands preeminent the means at the Council's disposal for influencing the law courts. These were various. In some instances the King transferred to the Star Chamber cases on which the courts were about to pronounce a decision. When this was done, it wanted but one more step for the King, as the phrase went, 'to take the matter into his own hands,' and, if he chose, pardon the offence, generally after a receipt of a large sum of money. Instances abound in Henry VII's reign, where criminals escaped justice by bribing the monarch. Entries in the minutes, such as 'the Earl of Derby, for his pardon, £6,000;' 'for the pardon of William Harper,

---

[1] Proceedings of Privy Council, vii. 242.   [2] Ibid. vii. 246.

for treasons, felonies, escapes, and other offences, 2co marks;' which occur frequently in the Star Chamber's records, tell their own tale. Even if a pardon was not obtained, it was at times an advantage to be tried in the King's own court. A murder, for example, if put on trial in the Star Chamber, since it was not within the Council's competence to inflict death, was sure to escape with a penalty less than that which the law assigned. An instrument by which the Crown weighed down the freedom of the courts was by summoning juries before the Council, to account for their verdict. They were, indeed, at liberty to give a true verdict, according to the evidence, but it was well for them if their view of truth coincided with the opinion of the government; for, if otherwise, they were liable to be taught their duties by a summons before the Star Chamber, and a summons which frequently was followed by fines, and by imprisonment. 'I have seen, in my time,' writes the author of the Treatise on the Commonwealth[1], 'that an inquest, for pronouncing not guilty of treason, contrary to such evidence as was brought in, were not only imprisoned for a space, but a large fine set on their heads, which they were feign to pay.' This statement places beyond a doubt the fact that juries were punished for their

---

[1] Commonwealth of England, book iii. cap. 1. Hallam's Const. Hist. (8th ed.), i. 49.

verdict, and raises the suspicion that of the 'forty jurymen convicted within a year of perjury,' mentioned by Hudson, some were as much martyrs to love of justice as perjurers.

Right of inflicting torture. It was not always to oppose the law courts that the Council put forth its powers. It sometimes gave them help, but it was aid of a peculiar kind. The law of England has always forbidden the use of tortures. Numerous lawyers have pronounced it illegal. Yet there is the most abundant proof that torture was used in England till 1640[1]. The only body who employed it were the Councillors, and they were always ready to do for the law courts what the judges dared not do for themselves. Whenever a great crime had been committed, the Council did its best to force out truth by the rack. A long list of cases shows, that to inflict tortures was the daily habit of the Crown's advisers. The names of Anne Askew and Guy Fawkes recall the best known examples of the employment of torture in obedience to a royal order. Repulsive as this exercise of the Crown's authority sounds to modern ears, it was not considered strictly illegal. Sir Thomas Smith, who denounces the use of torture, was himself present at its employment; and this circumstance, combined with some others, is a valid proof that to torture subjects was in the

[1] Gardiner, Hist. of Eng. ix. 141.

sixteenth century held to be a prerogative of the Crown. This privilege, if so it can be called, throws some obscurity over particular branches of the Council's judicial action, since it renders it doubtful whether some minor crimes were brought to the Star Chamber for trial, and not rather for examination. Various royal orders testify to the readiness with which the King ordered the employment of the rack; and a more indelible proof of this than written mandates can afford, is to be found on the stones of a dungeon, within the Tower, where those who care may still read how—

> 'Thomas Miagh which lieth here alone,
> That fayne wolde from hens begon,
> By torture strange my trouth was tryed,
> Yet of my libertie denied.
>   1581, THOMAS MIAGH[1].'

Yet if the right to inflict agony was the most fearful, it was far from being the most dangerous privilege of royalty which was exercised by the Star Chamber. This court, not content with Civil suits. criminal jurisdiction, attempted to interfere with the rights of property. Its endeavours were, as may be seen from examples in the Council's Records[2], at first successful. Nevertheless, for some reason which does not seem to be entirely explained, it paid less and less

---

[1] Jardine Reading on the Use of Torture, p. 30.
[2] Proceedings of Privy Council, vii. 58, 214, 276.

attention to civil suits, until under Charles I an attempt was made to revise the jurisdiction in civil causes.

The Councillors, in addition to the authority which they claimed as members of a powerful court, assumed to themselves a further right of a most oppressive nature. They pretended, not merely collectively as the Council, but individually as Councillors, to possess the privilege of arresting their fellow-citizens. The ultimate defence of such an arrest would have been, it must be supposed, the plea of obedience to a royal command. Nevertheless, the Councillors claimed (though doubtless under responsibility to the Crown) to act in this matter on their own judgment. Their claim is itself sufficiently strange, but it is stranger still to find, that to some extent the Judges admitted its validity, at least as regards the Council collectively. 'We think,' say the Judges of 1591, in a formal document drawn up as a protest against illegal commitments, 'that if any person shall be committed by Her Majesty's special commandment, or by order from the Council board, or for treason touching Her Majesty's person, ... which causes being generally returned into any court is good cause, for the same court to leave the person committed in custody [1].'

Some of the main features of the 'government

Councillor's right to arrest.

---

[1] Hallam's Const. Hist. (8th ed.), vol. i. 236.

by Councils,' as it existed under the Tudors, have now been roughly sketched. It is worth while to cast back a glance at the general picture presented. For it is only when looked at as a whole that the strangeness of the system can be comprehended. The Council stands forth, as at the same moment, powerless and powerful. In its dealings with the Crown it is utterly weak, for it has lost every element of independence. In its dealings with the people it is irresistibly strong, for it combines every element of authority. The ablest administrators of the day are its members. The political powers which it exercised in the fifteenth century remain (except in reference to the King) unimpaired, and to these powers has been added all the authority of a law court, and nearly all the influence of a legislative assembly. Above all, the whole body is subject to one head. The King is all in all: and the Tudor princes were exactly the chiefs which the Council required; for, with many faults, they combined an appreciation of talent which made them appoint able Ministers, with a love for business, which enabled them to keep in motion the cumbersome machinery of government, of which they themselves were the creators.

It is at this point of history that the question is most fairly asked, did the scheme of government, of which the Council was the embodiment, prove truly successful? To put the same inquiry in another form, were the great powers, centred in the hands of the executive government, exercised for the national benefit? The answer to these questions, if it is to be a true one, must be to some extent undecided. The Council's rule had great merits. It gave a splendid field for the exercise of administrative ability. The rule of Henry VIII and Elizabeth afforded to a greater extent than any other English government, a noble career for men of talent. Their strong rule conferred great benefit on the nation. It carried the country with success through both a religious and a social crisis. It brought about, moreover, a century of more profound internal peace than England had ever before enjoyed. These blessings, however, were counterbalanced by gigantic evils. The rule of the Tudors was in the main a selfish rule. Where the interests of the Crown and of the people coincided the government acted with patriotism. Where they differed, everything was sacrificed to the interest of the King. Great Ministers were promoted; yet Cromwell, the greatest of them all, was judicially murdered. Law was enforced; but law itself was made, under Henry VII, a means of sordid gain, and under his son, of despotic power. The Church was purified, but it was also plundered. Even under Elizabeth, members of the Council were

Under the Tudors mixed.

guilty of shameless rapacity. Cecil and Hatton grew rich on Church spoils, and bishoprics were left unfilled, that courtiers or the Crown might appropriate the proceeds of the see. If order was restored, liberty was destroyed. The courts were subservient, and the Council overawed the feeble independence of the courts. The system of government, founded by Henry VII, was tottering to its fall ere his granddaughter's death ; and those, if any there be, who regret the decline of the Council's power, may see in the petition of Elizabeth's judges the description of the tyranny which that power entailed. ' We beg,' say the guardians of justice, 'that Her Majesty's subjects be not committed or detained in prison, by the command of any nobleman or Councillor, against the laws of the realm, to the grievous charge and oppression of Her Majesty's said subjects. Some parties so committed, after they had been lawfully discharged in court, have been soon recommitted to prison, in secret places, so as upon enquiry the Queen's court cannot learn to whom to award Her Majesty's writ, without which justice cannot be done[1].'

In the celebrated statute 16 Car. I, cap. 10, (1640), it is placed on record, that 'the reasons and motives for the erection of the Court of Star Chamber do now cease.' This assertion might

[1] Hallam's Const. Hist. (8th ed.), i. p. 224.

with truth have been given a much wider extension, for it applied as much to the whole system of administration, which had existed for a hundred and fifty years, as to the Star Chamber, which was only the most prominent part of a closely connected body of institutions. From the moment when James ascended the throne, a revolution of one kind or another was inevitable. With the last of the Tudors ought to have expired the Tudor system of government. Nominally it survived, for in form the Council of James and Charles was like that of Elizabeth. Since, before her death, had taken place one change in its internal constitution, by which Cecil had passed from mere Secretary into Secretary of State. The alteration of title is of no moment in itself, but has importance as being the official recognition of the place occupied by a Minister, whose duties were undefined, and who had, in early times, no seat at the Council board. Nevertheless, the Tudors' system, was, if not dead, at least dying. The Stuarts might have ruled with more skill. They might have been the leaders of a reform, instead of becoming the victims of a revolution. No policy, however, could have long averted some alteration in the government.

Under the Stuarts it failed.

The stronghold of the preceding race of monarchs had been the Council; that is, the combination of all the powers of the state in the hands of a considerable number of Ministers. In 1603, this system was already doomed, for the state of things which produced it had passed away. The country, which in 1485 was exhausted by wars, was at the beginning of the seventeenth century restored to vigour and prosperity, through a long peace. The anarchy, which Henry VII reduced to order, had given place to a spirit of tranquillity and repose. The law courts were sufficiently strong to perform their duties, and had more reason to dread than to court the aid of the executive. No danger of foreign invasion, or peril from domestic conspirators, made a strong government a national want. For the Gunpowder Plot marked rather the weakness than the strength of the Roman Catholics, and in the difference between the 'Pilgrimage of Grace,' under the leadership of nobles, and the November conspiracy, planned by insignificant country gentlemen, and carried out by assassins, may be seen the whole interval which separated the Catholic party under Henry VIII from the Papistical conspirators under James I. At the precise moment when Superseded by Parliament. the Council's extraordinary powers became useless, they were overshadowed by the growth of Parliament. Government by Parliament and government by the Star Chamber were incompatible, though, perhaps, no one perceived them to be so, at the time of James's accession.

Moreover, the rule of the Council had never been undisputed. The lawyers of England have in modern times delayed many reforms; but the country owes them a debt of gratitude for their protests in past ages against arbitrary power. From them came the unceasing complaints of the Star Chamber's jurisdiction, of which the petition of the Judges in 1591 is an example. Under theories about the Star Chamber's origin, lay concealed a protest against its power. When Plowden asserted the Court's authority to be grounded on the statute of Henry VII, he gave currency to an historical error; but in doing so enunciated the political truth, that the Star Chamber's powers, if they did not rest on the Act 3 Henry VII, cap. 1, were founded not on law, but on unconstitutional encroachments of the Crown. Another prevalent opinion among lawyers was that (to use Hudson's words) 'the Star Chamber was no settled ordinary court of judicature, but only an assembly for consultation at the King's command, upon some urgent occasions, in cases where all other courts want power, for want of law to warrant them, and have no weight sufficient to poize the question.' This view nearly represents the historical facts of the case, and as surely as the theory of Plowden contains a protest against the Court's unconstitutional power.

It was not the opposition of lawyers, the change of popular feeling, or the growth of Parliament alone, which necessitated a change in the system of government. The Council was becoming unequal to its work. At the best it had been a clumsy instrument in the hands of the King. The Tudors had worked it, but not without difficulty. New requirements arose, and the Council was not a body fitted to meet them. Chief among these was the need of a regular army. In earlier times the necessity had not existed. But by the beginning of the reign of Charles I, it must have been evident to keen observers that it was impossible much longer to stave off the formation of a regular army; that when one was created, either the King or the Parliament must extend their power; and that whether the authority of the Crown or the liberties of the people were augmented, the form of government which had hitherto existed must come to an end. *And having become unequal to its work.*

The period, therefore, between the death of Elizabeth and the Restoration, may be considered as the time during which ' Government by Councils' fell. It is an apparent contradiction to this view, to assert that the Council's powers were never stretched so far as under James and his son. Nevertheless, both the assertion and the theory are true and consistent. The Council put forth all its powers during the reigns of the *Decline of the Council's real power.*

first two Stuarts, but these exertions of authority were signs of death. The Stuart kings acted, not with the consciousness of undisputed sway which distinguished Henry VIII, but under a strong, though it may be unconscious feeling, that their power was in danger and needed to be increased, if it was not to be lessened.' Hence all the acts of their government are stamped with the impress of innovation. Few men perceived the true state of affairs, least of all Charles or his father. Stafford alone saw how matters really stood; and it is this clearness of view which gives to his policy of 'Thorough' a consistency which the Stuarts' other acts of tyranny want.

Not apparent at the time.

Though to an observer of a later age it appears manifest that from the time of James's accession the Council's struggles were the agonies of death, to an ordinary Englishman, living in 1603, it must have seemed far otherwise; for year by year the government's activity redoubled. James not only talked of the prerogative in language which Elizabeth would have felt to be unseemly, but wherever he could he carried out his theories into act. He, for instance, resumed the custom of the King's presiding at the Star Chamber's sessions—a habit which was as easily defended in theory as it was oppressive in practice. He levied customs without the assent of Parliament. He immensely stretched the force of proclamations. By these edicts he prohibited the manufacture of starch from wheat, and the erection of new buildings in London, whilst he also issued a decree that country gentlemen should at once leave town and return to their estates. The terrors of the Star Chamber were given full swing. Whitelock came before its bar charged with privately advising a client that a certain proclamation was illegal. A Mr. Fuller was imprisoned for life because he sued for a writ of Habeas Corpus for two Puritans, committed by the Court of High Commission. Selden was brought before the Council for the crime of publishing, in his History of Tithes, opinions offensive to High Church prelates. The use of torture was kept up, as is shown by the case of Peacham. Meanwhile, in reality, the Council's power declined. If the King talked in a new strain about the prerogative, the Parliament assumed a new tone about its privileges. As certainly as each Parliament met, so regularly the illegal acts of the Crown were denounced. Had James been able to dispense with Parliaments, the old system of government might have been for some time longer preserved. If he had held Parliaments, and kept within the law, the Council might have passed through a gradual process of change. He did neither. The Treasury was empty. The Tudors had gained little by having plundered the Church, for before

James's accession the plunder was spent. Moreover, the old sources of revenue from the feudal rights were running dry. Hence, James was driven to Parliament; but he had not the vigour to rule legally, and his whole reign was a series of encroachments which were checked, and of acts of tyranny, even more useless than oppressive. One circumstance sufficiently shows the great though silent crisis through which the country was passing. In 1614, James attempted to manage the Parliament. It took no great acuteness to foresee that the assembly which the Crown found it necessary to cajole was on the point of becoming the sovereign power of the state. A revolution, it was manifest, drew near; nevertheless, the plan of ruling by the Council lasted out James's time, and when in 1625 Charles mounted the throne, the Council was still an assembly with the same powers and the same constitution as it had possessed in 1603.

Silent Crisis.

A general review of Charles's reign has no place in the present essay. The period was one in which the Crown attempted a revolution, and dreamed it was carrying out a reaction. Hence the Council of Charles I was probably, in appearance, more like the Councils of the monarchs before Henry VIII than any which had existed since 1509. This resemblance was produced by the prominent position given to the Bishops, and by the number of nobles summoned to the board. The following list of Charles's Council in 1630, though it is imperfect, from only giving the names of Councillors who attended on two particular days, throws some light on the character of the King's advisers [1].

Sir Th. Coventry (The Lord Keeper).
Lord Weston (Lord Treasurer).
Earl of Pembroke (Lord Chamberlain).
Earl of Manchester (Lord Privy Seal).
Earl of Bridgewater.
Earl of Danby.
Earl of Kelley.
Earl of Arundel (Earl Marshal).

Viscount Wimbledon.
Viscount Dorchester.
Viscount Falkland.
Viscount Grandison.
Lord Newburgh.
Bp. of London (Laud).
Sir T. Edmunds (Mr. Treasurer).
Sir H. May (Mr. Vice-Chamberlain).
Mr. Secretary Coke.

This catalogue is suggestive. It exhibits not only the reaction in favour of the nobility, but also the Council's immense decline in administrative talent, since the days of the Tudors. Their Ministers were Cromwells, Cecils, Walsinghams. The administrators of Charles's government were Pembrokes, Westons, Bridgewaters. The list further suggests (though from its incompleteness it does not prove this) that the separation between the Privy Councillors and the ordinary Councillors had widened.

The most conspicuous acts of Charles's Council are too notorious to need more than a passing allusion. From the Council proceeded illegal demands for money. In the Star Chamber was

[1] Athenæum (1855), p. 1187.

found a means of punishing those who refused compliance. Chambers, in 1629, for the refusal to pay duties not imposed by Parliament, was summoned before the Privy Council [1]. On examination he gave expression to an opinion that in no part of the world, not even in Turkey, were merchants so 'screwed and wrung' as in England. To exhibit the falsehood of this assertion, the Star Chamber sentenced him to a fine of £2,000, and to make a humble submission. From the Council board came forth proclamations more arbitrary than even James had issued. They limited the importation of different articles [2], regulated trade, fixed the price of various commodities. The rights of property were no longer respected, since an edict of the Council commanded the demolition of buildings near St. Paul's, with or without the consent of the owners; whilst another mandate ordained that all the shops in Cheapside, except those of the goldsmiths, should be closed.

The Law courts, though subservient to the Crown, were not sufficiently servile to suit Charles's policy; and in 1631 the Council was empowered by a royal commission to 'examine and enquire into all differences which shall arise between any of the courts of justice [3],' and thus installed in a position to control all the proceed-

---

[1] Hallam's Const. Hist. ii. 7.
[2] Ibid. ii. 27.   [3] Ibid. ii. 9.

ings of the judicial tribunals. Each year the Council's encroachments became more oppres- sive, till from it issued the celebrated demand for ship money. The history of this demand, and of the resistance it met with, is known to every reader. Nothing is gained in a history of the Council by dwelling on the contest between the Crown and the people, which ended in the convocation of the Long Parliament.

One more example of the Council's despotic acts may close the list of its attacks on English freedom. The act is not one of outrageous tyranny, but it throws light on the state of England, and is remarkable from its connection with a celebrated name. In 1630, the Corporation of Huntingdon was remodelled. What was the ground on which the government claimed the right to interfere is not known. The object of the measure was alleged to be 'to prevent popular tumult, and to reduce the elections and other things, and the public business of the town, into certainty and order.' The effect of the measure was to establish a close corporation, and to excite discontent. Among those who gave expression to the general sentiment of dissatisfaction, was the future Protector. The Council's registers for November bear the record that Oliver Cromwell, esquire, and William Killburne, gentleman, having been formally sent

K

for by warrant, 'tendered their appearances
accordingly, which for their indemnities is entered on the list of the Council's causes, but they
are to remain in the custody of the messenger
until they shall be dismissed by their lordships.'
Cromwell and his accusers were examined on
the first of December[1]. The investigation led
to no result. An arbitrator between the two
parties dividing Huntingdon was appointed.
The town retained its new constitution, and
shortly after these events, Cromwell left Huntingdon for St. Ives.

Revolution
effected by
Long
Parlia-
ment.

Ten years after this examination took place, the
Long Parliament met. Its first measure was to
pass the Act 16 Car. I, cap. 10. This statute abolished the Star Chamber, and did away with
those judicial powers which the policy of a century and a half had grouped around the Council.
With the jurisdiction of the Star Chamber
vanished the power of those tribunals, which
under the name of Councils of the North, of
the West, had imitated the tyranny and increased the influence of the Privy Council. The
Long Parliament committed errors, and posterity
has dwelt more on its mistakes than on its
merits. Yet two deeds should have been alone
sufficient to have preserved the fame of the
patriots of 1640. Their noblest achievements
were the establishment of the rule of regular

[1] Athenæum (1855), p. 1187.

law, and the abolition of torture. The single
assertion made by a careful enquirer, that after
1640 no instance can be discovered of torture
being employed, is the Long Parliament's highest
eulogy.

The restoration of the Stuarts and the restor- Compari-
ation of the Bourbons have been made the son of
French and
subject of many antithetical comparisons. The English re-
volutions.
French royal family, it is said, returned to a
nation where everything had been changed,
whilst the Stuarts came back to a land where
nothing was altered. Had this contrast not
possessed some appearance of truth, it could
never have become trite from repetition. Reflection, however, shows that the amount of truth
which it contains is small, and the view of
history on which it rests one-sided. The reader
who has learnt that the revolution of 1640 produced no permanent change, must be perplexed
to account for the feeling which every one enter-
tains, that from the time of the Restoration
English history has an entirely modern tone,
whilst in the age of Charles I there remains a
strong tinge of mediævalism. The coexistence
of the common notion, that the Restoration
brought matters back to the point at which they
stood before the civil wars, together with the
apparently contradictory feeling that from 1660
commences a modern era, is accounted for by the
slight . attention which has been paid to the

history of the Council. Leave this body out of consideration, and it may with truth be said that the Long Parliament affected no permanent alterations. What the Church was under Charles I, such, in form at least, it continued to be under Charles II. The Parliament which welcomed back Charles in 1660, had the same constitution as the Parliament which greeted James on his accession in 1603. No great social change had been worked by the leaders of the Commonwealth. The Levellers had been arrested in their course, and landed property had not changed hands during the rule of the Protector. Let, on the other hand, the altered position of the Council be taken into account, and the work done by the men of 1640 stands forth in all its greatness. Their schemes of Church reform, their attempts directly to curtail the Crown's power, came to nothing. Yet they

Effect of Star Chamber's destruction.

had not lived and laboured in vain. The power of the Star Chamber had been thrown to the ground; and, with its fall, the whole system of government was changed. The struggle for liberty was not ended, but it had entered on a new phase. Disputes about the Council's rights were done away with for ever. The Councillors had formed a barrier between the Parliament and the Crown. The barrier was removed, and the two powers of the state were brought face to face, to finish the struggle for sovereignty. This contest was not finally decided till 1688; but its decision then would not have been possible had it not been for the reforms of the Long Parliament.

'Restauration ist immer auch Revolution,' is the dictum of the most recent enquirer into Roman history. The saying holds good of the English Restoration. No more loyal assembly ever met than the Parliament of 1660. It was eager to undo the work of the last twenty years. At one point, however, it held its hand. A proposition was made to restore the Star Chamber. Loyalty forbad that the proposal should be rejected, but it was allowed to come to nothing. The Parliament itself could hardly have told what was the reason which made it hesitate at this particular measure. It paused in the work of reaction, not so much from any dictate of respect for liberty as from that species of instinct which will at times make patent to a whole people that a particular law or institution is become a thing of the past.

Moreover it may be conjectured that the Parliament was not thoroughly aware of the revolution which the abolition of the Star Chamber involved. The House of Commons probably conceived that they had merely cut down abuses which had clustered around an ancient institution, and had restored the government to the form which it had held before the rise of the

Not fully understood by Parliament.

Star Chamber's authority. In appearance this had been done: for the Council's political powers remained uncurtailed. It was in 1660, as it still is in 1860, the only body of royal Ministers known to the law. Nevertheless Parliament, in cutting down its judicial power, had not lopped off an accidental outgrowth on the original constitution of the Council, but had taken away the essential characteristic which had given to the Privy Council its peculiar nature. It had at all former periods been an assembly of all the greatest officers of the state. It was rather the case that the officers made up the Council than that from the Council were appointed the officers. Each Minister was responsible for his own department, while for the general policy of the government he had no necessary responsibility. What course of action the government should pursue was decided, in most cases, by the King himself; in others (as for instance during a minority), by the majority of the Council. The whole assembly had not, nor was supposed to have, an united policy. In many cases, during the fifteenth century, different Councillors opposed each other with as much freedom as in modern days the head of the Ministry and the leader of the opposition. During the whole minority of Henry VI, Beaufort and Gloucester attacked one another with all the bitterness to be expected from the chiefs of opposite factions. Under the Tudors, this species of opposition between members of the Council ceased, not because the Councillors agreed together, but because each Minister had little to do but to transact the affairs of his department, in obedience to the monarch's will. In an assembly where the members had no need to agree together on matters of policy, smallness of numbers was not required. The Council of Edward VI consisted of forty persons, but there is no reason to suppose that the Councillors agreed in anything but in readiness to carry out the King's behests. The 'committee for the state' were perhaps agreed on general principles of policy, but they made up a number little larger than that of a modern Cabinet.

The Parliament of 1660 had made the Council a purely political body. Among its members were still included the great officers of state; but for the business which it had to transact the presence of many of these great officials was no less inconvenient than unnecessary. There was, for instance, no reason of propriety or convenience for calling on the Archbishop of Canterbury to attend at debates about questions of foreign affairs, or of court intrigues. Moreover, from different reasons, the King and the Parliament agreed in the desire to substitute a smaller body for the Council. Charles hated the formality of long discussions, and felt with

reason that (to quote from his own declaration of
1679) a Council was 'unfit for the secresy and
despatch which are necessary in great affairs.'
The Parliament entertained the feeling that
Ministers ought to be responsible, and ought to
Inevitable pursue some definite policy.   If the whole Coun-
change cil were really the Ministry, this could not be.
It was a body too numerous to agree together,
or to be made responsible for its political acts.
Some change was felt to be necessary, whilst no
one knew exactly what it ought to be.   A
democratic assembly would have attempted to
appoint the Crown's Ministers directly by Parliament.   Something of this kind the Long
Parliament had endeavoured to achieve.   Before
the arrest of the five members, Charles I bound
himself to act by the advice of two or three
persons, acceptable to the House of Commons ;
that is, to form a Ministry : and the propositions
of Newport contained the stipulation that Parliament should nominate the King's Council.
Plans such as these met with no acceptance in
the eyes of assemblies inspired with the loyalty
of the Restoration.   Innovation was their horror.
They still looked on the Privy Council as the
regular Government, and meditated no change
in its constitution.

came from   The alteration which was inevitable came
the Crown. from the side of the Crown.   Clarendon laments,
with some bitterness, Charles II's dislike to

debates in Council. The Chancellor saw that more and more the habit of consulting the whole body of the Councillors was going into disuse, and that the arbitrary power which Charles coveted was the authority of a Louis XIV, not of a Henry VIII. He saw the change in progress; he perceived the great evils which it involved: he did not understand that these perils could only be met by other changes in the constitution of the country. The alteration was one impossible to oppose, for Charles altered not a single point in the form of the Council. He changed its character by making use of one of its peculiar characteristics. Since at all times the Council had acted through committees, the King could, without any innovation, form a special committee, or (to use a term in use even in his father's reign) a 'Cabinet,' to which alone the secrets of his policy were confided. This body in reality, though not in name, superseded the rest of the Council. The whole body of Privy Councillors, as from this point they may be termed, were either never consulted or only consulted when it was too late for their advice to be more than a formality. In connection with the formation of a Cabinet, Charles greatly increased the number of the whole Council; and thus obtained a valid reason for employing only a select body of his advisers. His proceedings are clearly described in his own declaration of 1679:—

'His Majesty thanks you (the Councillors) for all the good advices you have given him, which might have been more frequent if the great number of this Council had not made it unfit for the secresy and despatch that are necessary in many great affairs. This forced him to use a smaller number of you in a foreign committee (the Cabal), and sometimes the advices of some few among them upon such occasions, for many years past.'

The formation of a Cabinet was a necessity which, while unaccompanied with other changes, was fraught with great evils. It made all check upon the King through the Council a mere sham. It made men the real governors of the country who were not the governors in name, and who scarcely could be made responsible for their acts. A later age discovered a remedy for these evils, through transferring to Parliament, by a very circuitous process, the nomination of Ministers. This remedy was brought about by indirect means, and through a combination of circumstances which no wisdom could have foreseen. There is, therefore, no cause to wonder that thoughtful men, who saw the Council gliding into a Cabal, felt the danger of a change which they knew not how to avert. In 1679 the whole of this peril was apparent. A Parliament had met, more hostile to the Crown than any which had assembled since 1640. Long misgovernment had irritated the whole people. The name of the Cabal had become a bye-word, and the phantom of the Popish plot terrified the nation to madness.

No man lived with greater claims to the title of a philosophic statesman than Sir W. Temple. The King applied to him for advice. The requested advice was at once given, and consisted in a plan for the reconstruction of the Council. The plan is minutely detailed by Temple himself. It was nothing less than an ingenious attempt to combine the advantages of the old system of government by a Council, with the merits of the modern plan of government by a Cabinet, formed from the principal Parliamentary leaders of the day. A new Council was created, consisting of only thirty persons. Among them were the Archbishop of Canterbury, the Bishop of London, the Treasurer, the Lord Chancellor, &c. So far, the Council as planned by Temple was a mere revival of the Council which had advised the Tudors. Three new ideas gave originality to his scheme. The first was, that the Council should, as it were, represent the different influential bodies of the nation. Thus the bishops are 'to take care of the Church.' The Lord Chancellor and the Chief Justice are to 'inform the King well of what concerns the laws.' The second is the admission of influential members of Parliament.

Temple's scheme.

The last, that the Council should derive weight from its collective property. Temple's own words warrant confident assertions as to the nature of the institution which he planned. 'It seemed necessary,' he writes, 'to take into the Council some lords and commoners, who were of most appearing credit and sway in both houses, without being thought either principled or interested against the government, and mix them up with others of His Majesty's more general choice, for the making up of one half of the Council, whilst the other half were ever to be the present chief officers of his crown and household. .... But one chief regard necessary to this constitution, was that of the personal riches of this new Council, which in revenues of land and offices was found to amount to about £300,000 a year, whereas those of a House of Commons are seldom found to have exceeded £400,000. And authority is observed much to follow land, and at the worst, such a Council might of their own stock, and upon a pinch, furnish the King so far as to relieve some great necessity of the Crown[1].'

Temple's plan, in spite of its ingenuity, utterly failed. Within two years he had retired from office, filled with disgust and mortification, and his scheme had passed away as completely as any other paper constitution, which philosophers

[1] Temple's Memoirs (1720), p. 233.

have drawn up, and politicians have refused to adopt. He attributes his failure to the King's duplicity, and to the admission of Shaftesbury to the Council Board. The King, doubtless, had made a tool of the philosopher. But the reason of Temple's failure lay much deeper than any causes which he assigns. His Council was too much or too little. It was too large for a Cabinet, too small for a Parliament. It represented two inconsistent principles: appointment of Ministers for the sake of their Parliamentary influence, and appointment of Ministers because they were acceptable to the King. If the first principle was to be adopted, the King was right in admitting Shaftesbury. If the second, he made an error in sending for Temple. It was in vain the Chancellor blessed Temple's scheme as 'a thing from heaven fallen into His Majesty's heart,' that Sunderland gave his hearty approval, and Essex burst forth into hyperbolical eulogy. The plan was doomed to failure from its birth. The Parliament received it coldly, and had reason to do so, since, on Temple's own admission, the authority of his Council was meant to counterbalance the influence of Parliament. Bickerings broke out among the Councillors, and Temple dealt a death blow to his own creation, when, though the essence of his scheme was that all the Council should be consulted, he consented to form part of a Council within the

Reasons why it failed.

Council. It is, however, from its very inconsistencies, that Temple's plan derives interest.

It marks the transition from government by the whole Council to government by a Cabinet. For from 1679 no systematic attempt has been made to render all the Privy Councillors responsible for the Crown's political acts. In the original Act of Settlement, an enactment was introduced which had this tendency, but it remained a dead letter, and was shortly afterwards repealed. The growth of the Cabinet was, however, a gradual process. The Council is still the only body of royal Ministers known to the English law, and it was long before the people generally recognized the fact, that the Privy Council was not in reality the government of the realm. It long continued to be the custom to convoke the Privy Council on important occasions, such as the signature of the Peace of Utrecht. But the convocation was a mere formality, since Ministers had decided what was to be done, before the Council met. This useless form, which could have no other effect than to diminish the responsibility of the Crown's real advisers, has now been dropped. Yet, down to a late period, the Cabinet was looked upon as an anomaly. A writer of 1701 lays down the principle, that 'in setting the seal to foreign alliances the Chancellor has a safe rule to follow ; that is, humbly to inform His Majesty that he cannot legally set the great seal to a matter of that consequence unless the same be first debated and resolved in Council.' In 1711 an objection was made in Parliament to the term 'Cabinet Council,' as an expression unknown to our law ; and Lord Peterborough could describe the Privy Council as a body 'who were thought to know every thing and knew nothing,' and the Cabinet Council as those 'who thought nobody knew any thing but themselves.' In truth the Cabinet is an anomaly, though it is one with which custom has made the present age so familiar that its strangeness is forgotten. In theory the Cabinet is nothing but a committee of the Privy Council, yet with the Council it has in reality no dealings ; and thus the extraordinary result has taken place, that the Government of England is in the hands of men whose position is legally undefined : that while the Cabinet is a word of every-day use, no lawyer can say what a Cabinet is : that while no ordinary Englishman knows who the Lords of the Council are, the Church of England prays, Sunday by Sunday, that these Lords may be 'endued with wisdom and understanding !' that while the collective responsibility of Ministers is a doctrine appealed to by members of the Government, no less than by their opponents, it is more than doubtful whether such responsibility could be enforced by any legal penalties : that, to sum up this catalogue of

The Cabinet really an anomaly.

contradictions, the Privy Council has the same political powers which it had when Henry VIII ascended the throne, whilst it is in reality composed of persons many of whom never have taken part or wished to take part in the contests of political life.

The Act 16 Car. I, cap. 10, had taken away the Council's extraordinary judicial powers, yet some regular judicial authority it still retained. It exercised the right of arresting and examining accused persons, whom it afterwards sent to the regular Law Courts. It constituted a court of appeal from the colonial and the ecclesiastical tribunals. Its authority in these cases was open to no objection, for appeals were in fact referred to law officers, and settled with the same attention to law as suits in Chancery. Even these vestiges of the Council's ancient jurisdiction have been taken away by the Act 3 and 4 Will. IV, for this measure transfers the judicial powers of the Council from the whole body; who, however, did not in fact exert them, to a special committee. Thus statute has produced the same effect on the Council's legal authority which custom has had on its political powers. In each case the functions of the whole body have passed into the hands of a smaller committee, connected with the Privy Council by little more than its name.

There are, however, many powers still exer-

End of Council's government.

ciscd, nominally at least, through the Privy Council. Many of these are conferred by statute. To the Queen in Council is at times left the decision whether a given act shall be put in force; to the decision of the Queen in Council, for example, was left the date at which the Divorce Act should come into operation. Other rights, such as those of proclaiming ports, or fairs, fall to the Council as the only legal medium through which the Crown can exert its prerogatives. These powers, insignificant in themselves, clearly exhibit the position in which the Council stands. Through Privy Councillors, and through them alone, can the Monarch act; and hence the powers of the Crown are in a sense the powers of the Council. They have risen, they have flourished, they have declined, together. They are each vague and undefined. They are each encircled with the halo of antiquity, and point to a past greatness of which the might has departed without taking away the dignity.

Powers of Council really powers of the Crown.

A recent writer has said, that nothing is more interesting than to trace the history of a great cause; and that as the enquirer contemplates its rise from small beginnings, its difficulties, its progress, or its failure, he feels a sort of personal interest in the varying fate of a great principle. Something similar is experienced by those who mark the history of a great institution. An interest by degrees awakens in the institution

Conclusion.

L

itself. It seems to have a life, an individuality, a destiny of its own. It is the creation of man, but it is greater than its creators, for it lives on while they perish. Yet, the work of man, it too is mortal; and meets with disease, decline, and death. If any institution can claim a sympathy, generally accorded rather to human beings than to their works, the Council of the English monarchy may demand our especial interest. It boasts a history stretching back to remote antiquity. It acquired power amidst all the dangers of a barbarous age. For a long period it contained all that was noblest in English political life. The Beauforts, the Bedfords, the Cromwells, the Cecils, and Walsinghams of England, found within it at once the sphere and the reward for their talents. The benefits which it conferred in periods when it was the real protector of the weak, the true 'poor man's court,' more than counterbalance the evils which it produced when in later ages it rose as the Star Chamber, to be the most oppressive authority which ever threatened the liberties of England.

Whatever be the amount of sympathy which the Council shall command, its history will be found the more instructive the more carefully it is studied: for that history is nothing else than the account of the rise of all the greatest institutions which make up our national constitution. Our Parliaments and our Law Courts are but the outgrowth of the Council. In its history is seen how not only institutions but ideas assumed their modern form. As we study the gradual separation of judicial, political, and administrative functions, it is perceived that the notions of 'Law,' 'the State,' and 'the Government,' which now are so impressed on men's minds as almost to bear the delusive appearance of innate ideas, themselves grew up by slow degrees; and that the annals of a past age can never be understood till men have ceased to apply to them terms and conceptions which are themselves the product of later periods.

4